>>>>>>>>>> HOW TO BE A >>>>>>>>>>

# PRO GAMER

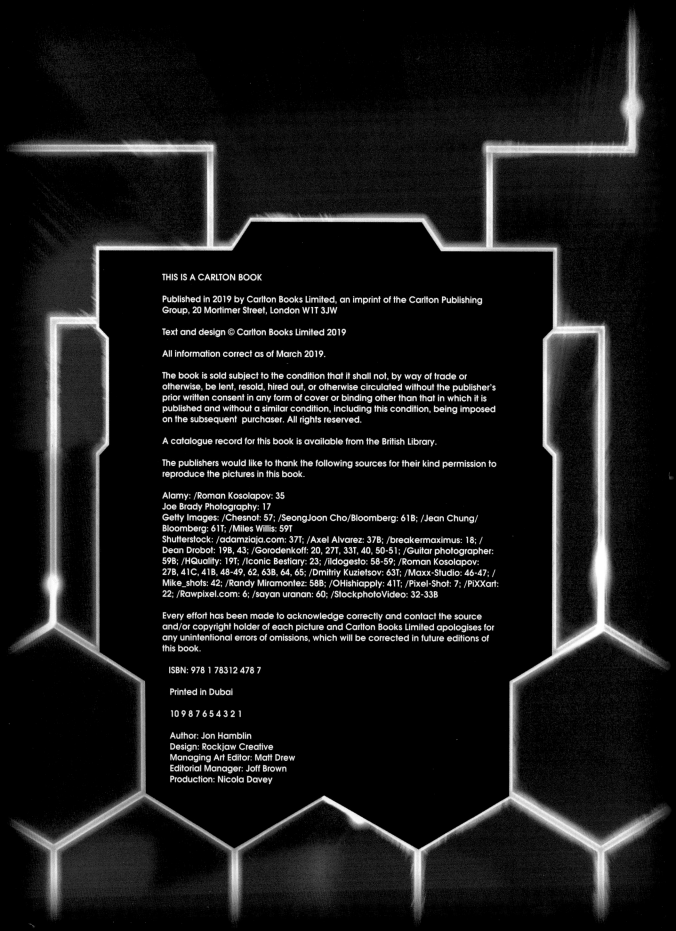

THIS IS A CARLTON BOOK

Published in 2019 by Carlton Books Limited, an imprint of the Carlton Publishing Group, 20 Mortimer Street, London W1T 3JW

Text and design © Carlton Books Limited 2019

All information correct as of March 2019.

A catalogue record for this book is available from the British Library.

The publishers would like to thank the following sources for their kind permission to reproduce the pictures in this book.

Alamy: /Roman Kosolapov: 35
Joe Brady Photography: 17
Getty Images: /Chesnot: 57; /SeongJoon Cho/Bloomberg: 61B; /Jean Chung/ Bloomberg: 61T; /Miles Willis: 59T
Shutterstock: /adamziaja.com: 37T; /Axel Alvarez: 37B; /breakermaximus: 18; / Dean Drobot: 19B, 43; /Gorodenkoff: 20, 27T, 33T, 40, 50-51; /Guitar photographer: 59B; /HQuality: 19T; /Iconic Bestiary: 23; /ildogesto: 58-59; /Roman Kosolapov: 27B, 41C, 41B, 48-49, 62, 63B, 64, 65; /Dmitriy Kuzietsov: 63T; /Maxx-Studio: 46-47; / Mike_shots: 42; /Randy Miramontez: 58B; /OHishiapply: 41T; /Pixel-Shot: 7; /PiXXart: 22; /Rawpixel.com: 6; /sayan uranan: 60; /StockphotoVideo: 32-33B

Every effort has been made to acknowledge correctly and contact the source and/or copyright holder of each picture and Carlton Books Limited apologises for any unintentional errors of omissions, which will be corrected in future editions of this book.

ISBN: 978 1 78312 478 7

Printed in Dubai

10 9 8 7 6 5 4 3 2 1

Author: Jon Hamblin
Design: Rockjaw Creative
Managing Art Editor: Matt Drew
Editorial Manager: Joff Brown
Production: Nicola Davey

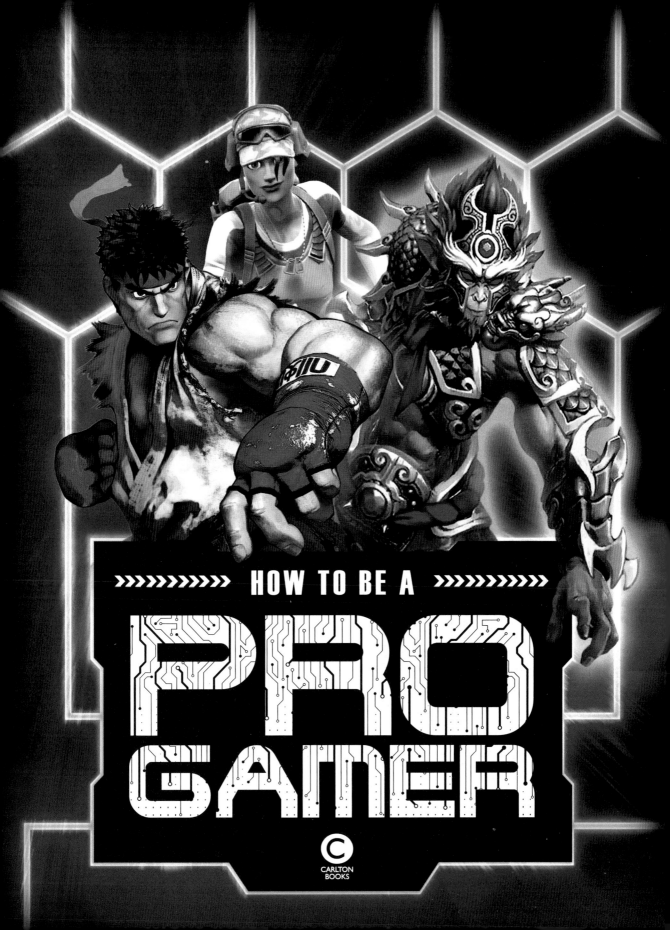

>>>>>>>>> HOW TO BE A >>>>>>>>>

# PRO GAMER

CARLTON
BOOKS

# CONTENTS

# GETTING STARTED

Whether you want to become a YouTube star, a Twitch clown or an eSports athlete, we're going to show you exactly how to blast your way to the top. Of course you'll need grit, determination, commitment (and the ability to headshot someone from 300 yards away) to get there, but if you follow this guide, you'll find your dreams are closer than you think. So let's get going!

# THE JOURNEY BEGINS

It's time to take your first step into the fast-paced world of pro gaming.
But you won't need a controller or keyboard just yet. It's prep time!

## THINGS YOU WILL NEED »»»»»»»»»»»»»»»»

**PEN**

**PAD**

**SNACK**

### Step 1: Research

The bad news is that the first step on any journey to becoming a Pro Gamer
is research. Lots and lots of research. The good news is, you've already
spent years doing it without even knowing it! Let's start by thinking of your
five favourite gaming personalities, then get out your notepad.

**1** Draw five columns down the page, and label the columns **NAME,
PERSONALITY, IMAGE, PROS** and **CONS**. (Or just use the space below.)

**2** Now go to your chosen personalities' pages on Twitch, Instagram,
YouTube, Twitter or Facebook, and start to fill in your columns.

| | – NAME –<br>Write their online name | – PERSONALITY –<br>Are they funny, intense,<br>knowledgeable...? | – IMAGE –<br>Have they got a cool logo,<br>or a nicely designed<br>header? | – PROS –<br>What do you love about<br>the personality? | – CONS –<br>What do you dislike<br>about them? |
|---|---|---|---|---|---|
| 1 | | | | | |
| 2 | | | | | |
| 3 | | | | | |
| 4 | | | | | |
| 5 | | | | | |

**3** You should now have a good sense of some
of the qualities that make for a good online
presence, and how it ties in with a personality type.

# Step 2: Creating a Persona

If you want to become a face on the pro gaming scene, there's nothing wrong with taking your most notable qualities and amping them up a bit.  For example:

If you're naturally funny, you might want to take on a more comic personality.

If you're all about the intensity of the battle, then bring that intensity to your persona.

If you like sneaking up behind people and hitting them with plastic chairs, then you should probably become a wrestler instead.

The most important thing is to pick a slightly exaggerated personality that's close enough to your own to be sustainable. If you're not sure what sort of personality fits you, try our 'Find your Gaming Identity' questionnaire on the next page.

## NAME INSPIRATIONS CHART

| FUNNY | SCARY | INTENSE | KNOWLEDGEABLE |
|---|---|---|---|
| Flip | Grim | Blunt | Sharp |
| Lit | Venom | Venom | Scientist |
| Kook | Livid | Hurricane | Verity |
| Wry | Nightmare | Punish | Certitude |
| Salty | Brutal | Smash | Master |
| Cheeky | Ravage | Epic | Gen |
| Gelastic | Crusher | Force | Brain |
| Frisky | Dread | Heavy | Theory |
| Antic | Demon | Hammer | Guru |
| Insane | Carnage | Power | Tech |

# FIND YOUR GAMING IDENTITY

If you're having difficulty working out exactly what sort of gamer you should be, then take this handy personality quiz! Pick one answer for each question, then add up your score at the end!

**1** You're at a tournament, and you see some cool-looking people to talk to. What's your opening line?

- **A.** "You like jokes? How about this one: Mario walks into a bar holding a large green pipe. Barman says 'Sorry sir, you can't smoke in here.'"
- **B.** "Have you seen Evo Moment #37? Daigo's a monster!"
- **C.** "Who wants a match? I'll take you all on singlehanded!"
- **D.** "Have you heard the good news about Satan, our dark lord and saviour?"

**2** You've just heard there's a re-make of your favourite retro game coming out, but it looks like they've botched it. How would you cover this news on your YouTube channel?

- **A.** A two minute video that replaces all the dialogue with fart noises.
- **B.** A thirty minute video comparing the upgraded textures and relative framerates.
- **C.** A one hour video demonstrating all the reasons why this remake is a TRAVESTY.
- **D.** A two hour video of you screaming in a black room.

**3** You've just lost a big match in a very public way. How do you respond to your victorious opponent?

- **A.** Offer them a high five and a smile.
- **B.** Congratulate them, then offer them a play-by-play of everything they did wrong.
- **C.** Immediately start complaining about the netcode and a faulty headphone cable.
- **D.** Start stabbing a crudely made effigy of them with a pencil.

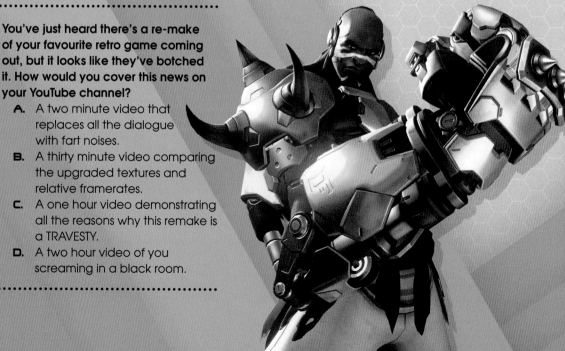

**4** You're living in a team house with other pro gamers, but your prized mouse has gone missing. You decide to write a note to your housemates. What does it say?

- ☐ **A.** "Guys, anyone got my mouse? Squeak now, or forever hold your cheese."
- ☐ **B.** "Free League of Legends coaching for anyone who can help find my mouse!"
- ☐ **C.** "Great. Now you've made me cry."
- ☐ **D.** "Return my mouse, or sleep with one eye open. Your choice."

**5** During a practice session you lay the smackdown on your team mate and they get upset. How do you cheer them up?

- ☐ **A.** Make them laugh.
- ☐ **B.** Show them that statistically, over the last 20 matches, they're still in the lead.
- ☐ **C.** Upset? Who's upset? *Continues to do victory fist pump*
- ☐ **D.** Offer to lend them your Ouija board, so they can chat with other people who are dead to you.

**6** You're streaming an F1 game. How's your driving?

- ☐ **A.** "Who likes bumper cars?!"
- ☐ **B.** "Fine, as long as I can hit this corner at a precise 31 degrees."
- ☐ **C.** "As long as I win, I'll be fine. Gotta go fast!"
- ☐ **D.** "Master demands a sacrifice - let's drive around the track the wrong way and see what happens!"

**7** What's the title of your first YouTube video?

- ☐ **A.** "Hairs of War: The 10 Worst 'dos in COD"
- ☐ **B.** "The Secret History of Sonic The Hedgehog"
- ☐ **C.** "How to be a Winner, Winner, Chicken Dinner"
- ☐ **D.** "Top 10 Occult References in Pokémon"

**8** You've just won your first tournament. Who do you dedicate the victory to?

- ☐ **A.** Your parents.
- ☐ **B.** Your PC.
- ☐ **C.** Yourself.
- ☐ **D.** Ialdagorth, the dark devourer.

**9** And what do you spend the prize money on?

- ☐ **A.** A Pikachu hat.
- ☐ **B.** Nolan Bushnell's autobiography.
- ☐ **C.** Energy drinks.
- ☐ **D.** A jar of eyeballs. Possibly real.

**10** You're just about to finish an epic 12 hour Overwatch streaming session. What's your final message to your fans?

- ☐ **A.** "Time to go - this D.Va needs her beauty sleep!"
- ☐ **B.** "TY! If anyone has any tips on increasing my DPS for Winston, let me know in the comments!"
- ☐ **C.** "We came, we saw, we crushed it! Until next time, true believers!"
- ☐ **D.** "HAIL SATIN! Arg, stupid autocorrect!"

## RESULTS

| | |
|---|---|
| Mostly A's | Just in it for the lols? You're clearly a funny gamer! |
| Mostly B's | With your cool head, and facts at your fingertips, you're a knowledgeable gamer! |
| Mostly C's | You feel every loss and wear your heart on your sleeve - you're definitely an intense gamer! |
| Mostly D's | Phew, you're definitely a scary gamer. Can you go stand over there now please? |

# WHAT'S YOUR GAME?

If you're going to be a gaming pro, you'll need to pick a speciality. Here's a guide to some of the different game genres to help you pick which game might suit you best...

## First Person Shooters

**Example Games:** Counter Strike: Global Operations, Halo 5, Overwatch
**Best For:** Eagle-eyed players
**Description:** First Person Shooters requires quick reactions, an awareness of your surroundings and a knowledge of maps second only to the Ordnance Survey. Just don't be a camper - no-one likes campers.

## Fighting

**Example Games:** Street Fighter V, Super Smash Bros. Ultimate, Tekken 6
**Best For:** Fast fingered players
**Description:** Fighting games are about more than just fast reactions and the ability to remember a million button combos. You also have to know the game's mechanics inside out, and learn how to read your opponent's moves. It's like playing chess, Mastermind and dodgeball while pulling off yoyo tricks at the same time. Tough stuff!

## Racing

**Example Games:** Gran Turismo Sport, F1 2018, Project CARS 2
**Best For:** Petrolheads
**Description:** Racing games are about more than just nudging other cars out of the way to get to the podium - you'll need to have a thorough understanding of physics, aerodynamics and engineering if you're going to win.

# Sports

**Example Games:** FIFA 2019, Rocket League, Madden NFL 19
**Best For:** Sports geeks
**Description:** If you love the roar of the crowd, and you like to get Messi with Ronaldo, then sports games are going to be your goal. While the balance between tactics and skill is different in most sports games, there's also a psychological element, as you read your opponents and find holes in their defenses.

# Battle Royale

**Example Games:** Fortnite, PlayerUnknown Battlegrounds, Call of Duty: Black Ops IIII
**Best For:** Survivalists
**Description:** Named after the cult film of the same name, Battle Royale games see you dumped into a large playing field that slowly reduces in size as players try to take each other out in an effort to be the last person standing. The ever-shrinking playfield makes it impossible to hide in one place for any length of time, and you'll need nerves of steel if you're ever going to earn that Winner, Winner, Chicken Dinner.

# Multiplayer Online Battle Arenas

**Example Games:** Dota 2, League of Legends, Heroes of the Storm
**Best For:** Tactical team players
**Description:** Multiplayer Online Battle Arena games usually involve trying to capture points on a map with your teammates. They require teamwork and a solid knowledge of what every character brings to the table. While the initial learning curve can be steep, the rewards are endless.

# Collectible Card Games

**Example Games:** Hearthstone, Clash Royale, Gwent, Shadowverse
**Best For:** Master tacticians
**Description:** Collectable Card Games are perfect for those that want to try their hand at games with a more relaxed pace. These games are all about building decks, and reading other players to gain an advantage. Deck building is not usually cheap though, and getting the exact cards you want can be time consuming.

# GEAR OF WAR

**Now you're all set to go, you're going to need some top-quality hardware. Here's our pick of the best current equipment.**

## THINGS YOU WILL NEED

CREDIT CARD

FRUIT JUICE

## Should I Build My PC?

Talk to any gaming pro, and they'll tell you that building your own PC is the only way to go. It's a rite of passage similar to building your own lightsaber, and no two are ever entirely the same. It also usually works out cheaper than buying an off the peg model. It is quite time consuming though, and if you're not technically-minded, it may prove quite a challenge, although there are thousands of websites, forums and YouTube channels to help you along the way. The build guides at https://pcpartpicker.com/ are a great place to start if you want to go down this route.

### BEST PC - ON A BUDGET

**DELL XPS TOWER SPECIAL EDITION**
**Features:** CPU: Intel Core i5-8400, Graphics: Nvidia GeForce GTX 1050 Ram: 8GB
**Cost:** From £799
**Review:** Although it may lack the sexy casings of some gaming PC's, the Dell XPS has got it where it counts. A great starter PC, it might not impress your friends with its looks, but they'll be blown away by its performance.

### BEST PC - MONEY NO OBJECT ▶▶▶

**CORSAIR ONE ELITE**
**Features:** CPU: Intel Core i7-8700K, Graphics: Nvidia GeForce GTX 1080 Ram: 32 GB
**Cost:** From £2799
**Review:** If you have the cash to splash, this near-silent god killer is the machine to get. It's compact, powerful and it looks like an alien artifact. Able to deliver 4K gaming without breaking a sweat, this is the ultimate buy.

### ◀◀◀ BEST MONITOR

**BENQ ZOWIE XL2540**

**Features:** Screen Size: 24", Resolution: 1,920 x 1,080, Aspect Ratio: 16:9, Response Time: 1ms

**Cost:** Approx £360

**Review:** There's no 4K support here, but the BenQ Zowie does have an ace up its sleeve - a phenomenally low refresh rate. This is all important when it comes to pro gaming, as even a couple of milliseconds can give you an advantage over your opponents.

### BEST MOUSE ▼▼▼

**STEELSERIES RIVAL 600**

**Features:** Dual sensors, optional additional weights, 3 side buttons

**Cost:** Approx £75

**Review:** This is one of the best products SteelSeries have put out in years. Featuring a bevy of side buttons, a 12,000 DPI sensor and enough LEDs to power a Daft Punk concert, this mouse will help you squeak plenty of victories.

### BEST KEYBOARD ▼▼▼

**FNATIC STREAK PRO**

**Features:** RGB backlighting, programmable layout, wrist rest

**Cost:** Approx £120

**Review:** Rubber-stamped by one of the best pro teams in eSports, the Fnatic Streak Pro is one of the best mechanical keyboards out there. Fully customisable, it's the perfect choice for gamers who want things exactly how they like them.

### BEST GAMEPAD ▲▲▲

**XBOX ONE CONTROLLER**

**Features:** Twin sticks, analogue triggers, Bluetooth, solid build

**Cost:** Approx £60

**Review:** Although there are other controllers out there, the Xbox One pad just feels good in your hands. It has some heft to it, and the sticks and triggers are extremely responsive.

### BEST HEADSET

**STEELSERIES ARCTIS PRO WIRELESS**

**Features:** Dual sensors, optional additional weights, 3 side buttons

**Cost:** Approx £299

**Review:** Combining wireless functionality with the crisp sound of the Arctis range, this is a great choice for calling out your plays. It also features a useful quick-swap feature for batteries.

### BEST GAMING CHAIR ▼▼▼

**SECRETLAB OMEGA**

**Features:** Memory foam cushions, tilt mechanism, lumbar support

**Cost:** Approx £75

**Review:** This stylish racing chair has everything you need - armrests, memory foam padding and decent lumbar support. Plus it's so comfortable, you can recline it back and have a quick snooze after the match...

# INTERVIEW#1:
# THE EDUCATORS

Digital Schoolhouse is a UK-based not-for-profit programme that runs the annual DSH eSports Tournament in schools and colleges in the UK. We asked Shahneila Saeed, their Programme Director, about the Digital Schoolhouse programme and how a career in games can fit in with school life...

### ▶ FOR THOSE THAT MIGHT NOT KNOW, WHAT IS DIGITAL SCHOOLHOUSE'S MISSION?

SHAHNEILA: Our mission is to revolutionise computing education in order to inspire the next generation. The programme uses play-based learning to engage pupils and teachers with the computing curriculum. So, it is not uncommon to drop into one of our workshops and see students learning programming concepts through magic and dancing or jigsaw puzzles and playdough!

### ▶ FOR GAMERS, A CAREER IN ESPORTS IS AN ATTRACTIVE PROPOSITION. IS IT A VALID CAREER PATH YET?

SHAHNEILA: eSports is an emerging sector in the UK with increasing opportunities for careers. Over 100 million viewers watch eSports via popular live streaming video platform Twitch a month. Likewise, the global audience is estimated to be in excess of 400 million viewers, with global revenues exceeding $700m and prize pools in the millions of dollars, eSports is a serious business.

### ▶ TELL US ABOUT THE DIGITAL SCHOOLHOUSE ESPORTS TOURNAMENTS, THAT YOU RAN IN ASSOCIATION WITH PLAYSTATION?

SHAHNEILA: Digital Schoolhouse National eSports Tournament is now in its third year. The 2017 - 2018 tournament saw 2222 students from 20 schools across the UK take part, and the 2019 tournament is already set to double in size, to almost 40 schools, reaching over 3500 children.

Students aged 12 - 18 participate not only as players but are also recruited to manage the tournament within their schools taking on valid industry roles such as event management, production, tournament administration, community management and on-screen talent.

### ▶ HOW DOES THE TOURNAMENT HELP STUDENTS?

SHAHNEILA: Creating a tournament which immerses students within the world of

▶▶▶ *Digital Schoolhouse tournament winners, proving that no matter what you might think, games aren't too cool for school.*

eSports has been a valuable way to get them to put into practice theory they have been learning in the classroom. The value of the skills that students developed whilst participating in the tournament is accredited by the Duke of York's iDEA Award. Post tournament, students were able to claim digital iDEA badges.

 **WHAT HAVE BEEN YOUR MAIN FINDINGS FROM RUNNING IT?**

SHAHNEILA: Over 80% of respondents said that the competition had increased their interest in participating in other team sports, and just under 90% said it had increased their interest in a career in the video games industry.

Improvements in confidence and student mental health were widely reported by the schools taking part.

 **PARENTS MIGHT HAVE SOME CONCERNS OVER THEIR KIDS WANTING TO PURSUE A CAREER IN ESPORTS. HOW WOULD YOU ADDRESS THOSE?**

SHAHNEILA: To be honest a lot of these concerns are there because eSports is likely to be unheard of amongst mums and dads.

As part of our eSports Tournament parents were invited to the Grand Final, and many said it was an eye opener for them. The Grand Final enabled the parents to not only hear from experts on our panel but also to speak with them and ask their questions for themselves, which went a long way to alleviate their concerns.

**IS IT HARD TO FIT ESPORTS AROUND SCHOOLWORK?**

SHAHNEILA: As with all things in life, achieving a balance is key. We've found that participation in the DSH Tournament can actually help to improve students' attendance. Results also suggest that it has helped increase student attainment.

**WHAT DOES THE FUTURE HOLD FOR ESPORTS IN GENERAL?**

SHAHNEILA: Anything is possible!

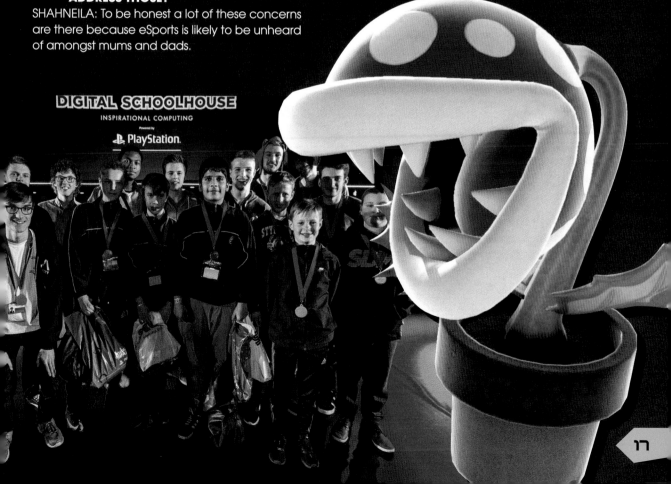

DIGITAL SCHOOLHOUSE
INSPIRATIONAL COMPUTING
Powered by
PlayStation.

# GET STREAMING

One of the easiest ways you can start to build your profile is by creating a good online presence. In this section, we're going to show you how to start your own YouTube and Twitch channels, and then how you can get the best out of them. Happy streaming!

TARGET ENGAGED

# FEELING TWITCHY

Since its arrival on the scene in 2011, Twitch has become the go to platform for gamers to play, chat and show off their skills. Twitch streamers broadcast their screens as they play, producing live video content for eager fans. So how can you get involved?

## THINGS YOU WILL NEED »»»»»»»»»»»»»»»

TWITCH
ACCOUNT

PC

ENERGY
DRINKS

## Step 1: Create Your Overlay

Once you've signed up for Twitch, you can create your first overlay. The overlay is the text and graphics layer that floats on top of your video content. It's designed to demonstrate your personality, give important information, and basically just look cool. You'll also need to create alert boxes, panels and screens, and these should all feature a consistent look.

### ART ATTACK

We recommend designing your own if you can, but if you're not particularly creative, you can buy off the shelf overlays that you can customise. Either way, you'll need an art package to create or edit it. Adobe Photoshop is probably the easiest professional package to use, although GIMP is a good free alternative.

# Overlay Example

1. **Channel name** - This is where the name of your channel goes. A cool logo would work well here.

2. **Social links** - So people know where they can find you elsewhere on the internet.

3. **Cam window** - This is where you'll appear. If your channel's primarily about entertainment, you'll want to make the cam window much bigger, so people can see you. If you're all about the gameplay, then you should make the cam window smaller.

4. **Top donator** - People love to get shout outs, and having a top donator shout out box will encourage people to donate greater sums of money.

5. **Latest donation** - Similar to the Top Donator shout out, this one gives everyone a brief mention.

6. **Latest follower** - Show your newest fan some love!

## Step 2: Assemble Your Studio

Before you can start broadcasting, you'll need some lighting equipment, a microphone or headset and a decent backdrop. See the next chapter for more information.

## Step 3: Start Streaming

Now you just have to put yourself out there and start streaming. Don't worry if your first steps are a bit wobbly - everyone needs time to learn. You probably won't be an overnight sensation either. But try to keep to a regular schedule, interact with your viewers and above all, have fun doing it, and the numbers will soon follow.

# DOWN THE TUBES

Although Twitch has become extremely popular for gamers, there's no denying YouTube's huge reach. You can create the videos at your own pace, and you can edit out any mistakes you make... as long as you learn the editing skills.

## THINGS YOU WILL NEED >>>>>>>>>>>>>>>

**YOUTUBE ACCOUNT**

**EDITING SOFTWARE**

**FRUIT**

## Step 1: Learn How To Edit

This could be an entire book by itself! But here's the basics. Editing is about re-organising footage to make it shorter and easier to understand. You can also use it to juxtapose images and sound in order to make points, i.e. adding a voiceover to your game footage. There are tons of free lessons on YouTube, or you could take a course at an online academy like Udemy.com.

### SOFTWARE

Final Cut Pro is the industry standard. Then you have Adobe Premiere, which is a bit more user-friendly, and reasonably affordable if you're a student. Adobe Premiere Rush is specifically designed for creating videos for social channels. If money's tight, apps like iMovie are more basic, but they'll get the job done.

## Step 2: Plan Your Content

It's always a good idea to know what you want to say before you make a video. When you have an idea, check around to make sure it hasn't already been done to death, and then come up with a cool, catchy title. This should be quite descriptive, so people know what they're about to see.

While it doesn't need to be fully scripted, it's a good idea to have all your talking points listed on a piece of paper that you can easily refer to. A strong beginning is key. People have short attention spans on YouTube!

## Step 3: Stay Regular

This applies to Twitching too, but keeping to a regular schedule is really important, whether it's daily, weekly or monthly. People want to know when new material is going to be out, and knowing that your videos drop every Tuesday at 5pm, will help you build an audience. Don't commit to too much at first - see what you can manage and then build it up over time.

# The Perfect YouTube Studio

1. PC - This is the centre of your world. The main unit is probably best tucked away under your desk to give you as much working space as possible.

2. Monitors - More than one is always good, to give you a larger gaming area, or to help you multitask.

3. Controllers - You'll need at least a mouse, a keyboard, a gamepad, and possibly other specialist controllers.

4. Gaming chair - Good lumbar support is important, because you'll be spending a lot of time sitting in this baby!

5. Lights - These will ensure you get plenty of light on your face evenly. Essential to looking professional in videos.

6. Microphone - A balanced arm or scissor stand will keep it in place, and a pop screen will eliminate any audible pops and clicks. If the room is echo-y, add some curtains and soft furnishings to soak up the sound.

7. Video camera - So that we can see your face!

# INTERVIEW#2:
# THE STREAMER

Streamers can bring games to life. We spoke to legendary streamer Dan "Foxdrop" Wyatt about his experiences with YouTube, Twitch and shoutcasting for League of Legends Championship Series (LCS).

### HOW DID YOU GET YOUR START IN GAMES?

DAN: Way back when I was a young kid with the Sega Megadrive that my dad had. He tells fond stories of me holding the controller staring at Sonic on the TV not realising I could control him. As I got older I got swept up in the Pokémon fad on Game Boy, and it continued from there.

### HOW DID YOU INITIALLY BUILD UP YOUR ONLINE FOLLOWING?

DAN: I got really good at League of Legends (top 0.1%), which was the most popular game at the time. I decided to make educational videos in my down time. I put these on Reddit and the League forums where they gained popularity. It sort of snowballed from there!

### HOW DOES SHOUTCASTING DIFFER FROM STREAMING?

DAN: Casting was a really random detour in my career, but a good one. I feel like the skills I gained in commentating my games on YouTube/streaming made the transition very easy. It's similar but different to regular streaming as I can focus more on the small details/entertainment and less so the actual gameplay.

### DO YOU THINK AN ONLINE 'PERSONA' IS NECESSARY, OR IS IT MORE IMPORTANT TO BE YOURSELF?

DAN: I think it depends, but I wouldn't say it's necessary. From what I've learned over the years having known many streamers, the persona is usually just a very extreme version of who the person is normally anyway.

### IS IT EASIER TO BUILD UP YOUR FOLLOWING IF YOU CONCENTRATE ON ONE GAME, OR IS VARIETY THE KEY?

DAN: In my opinion the optimal way to grow is to latch on to the most popular game so you have access to the widest audience. From there you can establish your brand and following, and people will be more likely to follow you to other games.

### IS IT POSSIBLE TO MAKE A LIVING JUST FROM STREAMING AND YOUTUBING?

DAN: Absolutely. It probably took a year or so for me to earn a living wage, but the great thing about this kind of stuff is that you can earn more and more as you grow.

### DO YOU FIND IT DIFFICULT TO KEEP UP WITH THE DEMAND FOR NEW CONTENT?

DAN: Yeah, that can be really tricky. Something that sticks with me is feeling like I could be making a video or streaming whenever I try to take time off. It's important to set good boundaries.

### HOW DO YOU DEAL WITH NEGATIVE FEEDBACK?

DAN: Most of the "hate" comments come from people who lack social skills, so often they sound harsher than they intend. Sometimes I will respond to these comments and the vast majority of times I will get a much nicer response back.

### WHAT'S BEEN YOUR FAVOURITE THING ABOUT HAVING AN ONLINE CAREER?

DAN: I'd have to say the ability to connect with people all over the world is a big one. The comfort of working from my own home is good too. And also the platform means I can talk about things other than just gaming, most specifically mental health stuff.

### WHAT'S YOUR TOP TIP FOR GAMERS WHO WANT TO GET INTO STREAMING?

DAN: Get good at the game and get a good set up, so the stream quality isn't awful. That's if you want to really go pro at streaming - if you just want to have fun with it, then just do it!

# BECOME AN ESPORTS STAR!

If you really want to kick your pro gaming career into the stratosphere, then eSports is where it's at. In this section we're going to teach you all the skills, strategies and knowledge you'll need to make it to the big leagues!

# GET GUD

If you're going to compete at a high level of play, you're going to need to get good at your chosen game. We mean REALLY good. So this week, you're going to start your training.

## THINGS YOU WILL NEED >>>>>>>>>>>>>>>>>>>>>>>>>>>

DIARY

FRIENDS

SPREAD-SHEET

## Step 1: Create a Practice Schedule

If you're going to succeed, you'll not just need to put in the hours - you'll need to devote yourself to learning everything about your chosen title.

Get a daily diary, and add at least three two-hour practice slots in a week. In these three practice sessions you'll be looking at three specific aspects of the game: Skills, Research and Tactics.

On top of this directed training, you'll probably be wanting to play somewhere around 30 hours a week - so make sure the game you pick is one you really enjoy!

### SKILLS

In these training sessions, you'll be looking to improve your base skills. These might include learning how to fast scope in an FPS, how to pull off a special move flawlessly in a fighting game, or how to take the perfect corner in a driving game.

### RESEARCH

This is your chance to learn every inch of the maps and tracks of your games, finding those secret nooks and crannies. Take this time to study YouTube videos and Twitch streams of competitive play, and try to observe the trick that the pros use.

### TACTICS

Tactics will always play a part in any game, and working out a good strategy for any situation will put you ahead of the pack. Think of yourself as a football coach, trying to work out the plays in advance.

## Step 2: Record Your Stats

After each game you play, record any relevant stats on a spreadsheet. You can use something like Google Sheets for this, as it's free. Write down your wins, losses, lap times, rounds taken to win - any statistic you can track.

You'll see these numbers gradually get better as you progress. If you play Overwatch, League of Legends, PUBG or Clash Royale, you can also upload your profile to a site like OP.GG to get an incredibly detailed breakdown of your stats.

# Step 3: Find your Sparring Partners

They say iron sharpens iron, and that's certainly true in competitive gaming. You'll need to find a group of people you can play with who are at or slightly above your playing ability. Keep playing them until you can beat them all easily, and then find newer, better players to play, and repeat the cycle. It's the only way you'll improve over time.

2:02    STOP THE PAYLOAD

▶ CONTESTED! ◀

# UPTOWN TOP RANKING

Once you've got a good feel for the basics, you'll need to make your way up to the big leagues. Which means making your way through the small leagues first. Most modern games have official routes to do this.

## Step 1: Have a Rank

Before you can get involved in ranked gameplay, some games will force you to complete an arbitrary amount of levels. This can differ in each game, but at the very least, most have some sort of tutorial to complete before you can start moving up through the ranks.

## Step 2: Points Mean Prizes

Once you've joined the rankings, you'll need to start working your way up. As you're new you'll find you probably lose as many games as you win. A 50% W/L ratio at this point is pretty decent - if you're winning more than that, then you're in great shape. Like most sports, many eSports games run in seasons. There can be anything from 1-4 seasons in a year, with points awarded to players at the end of each season.

**HOME IS WHERE THE HEARTH IS**

But how does it work in practice? Well, take Hearthstone. High rankings at the end of a season will earn you Hearthstone Championship Tour (HCT) points. Gain enough of these over a year, and you will be invited to the Hearthstone World Championship event. You can also supplement your points by attending and winning at official HCT events.

Other games have similar systems - Overwatch for example, has its Path To Pro System, which helps players move from their amateur Open Division through to their Overwatch Contenders programme, which in turn feeds the pro Overwatch League. Whichever game you're playing, make sure you understand how the various leagues and tournaments work, and then start working your way up. Remember, the more you play, the better you'll get, and the faster you'll climb the ranks.

# TEAM TITANS

If you're going to make it to the big leagues, you're going to need a team. Even if you play a game that's mostly solo, a team can give you emotional and financial support, as well as great advice.

## Step 1: Finding a Team

A team can be many things - it can be a group of players you enjoy playing with, it can be people you meet in the online community, or it can be an already established team. The two most important things are:

**1** You enjoy hanging out together - you're going to be spending a lot of time with each other, so make sure you actually enjoy each other's company!

**2** They're good practicing partners - this is really important, as you'll need to be in tune with each other, and knowing how they play will help you fight better and respect each other's calls.

Many tournaments will often help match you with other players, so don't worry if you're struggling to find people to team up with - someone you meet at a tournament could even be the start of a beautiful friendship.

## Step 2: Getting To Know You

Once you've established your team, you're going to need to start practicing together, so make sure your team mates are going to be around consistently. After all, there's no point having a team if you can never find time to actually play together. Create a schedule, and make sure everyone sticks to it!

# Step 3: Learn the Lingo

When joining a team, learning how to communicate is vital. While a lot of team chat is verbal, you may come across some slang while playing. Here's a guide to some of the more common expressions.

## LINGO

| WORD | MEANING |
| --- | --- |
| AFK | Away From Keyboard |
| ATM | At The Moment |
| BRB | Be Right Back |
| BUFF | Abilities need buffing |
| GG | Good Game |
| NERF | A weapon or ability is overpowered |
| NP | No Problem |
| NVM | Never Mind |
| RL | Real Life |
| TTYL | Talk To You Later |
| TY | Thank You |

# TEAM PLAYER

## THINGS YOU WILL NEED »»»»»»»»»»»»»»»»

Once you're part of a team, you're going to be spending a lot of time with each other. So how can you make sure you gel as a team?

BISCUITS

POST IT NOTES

CLEANING PRODUCTS

## Step 1: Learn the 7 Cs

Developed by top sports consultant Jeff Janssen, the 7 Cs are worth learning as they'll help your team pull together in the same direction. They are:

1. **Common Goal** - The team all need to be united behind a common goal. This can be winning a tournament, topping a league, or beating a rival team.

2. **Commitment** - The team need to be committed - if someone's consistently not pulling their weight, they need to go.

3. **Complementary Roles** - Every member of the team should bring something to the table that helps support the other players.

4. **Clear Communication** - This is key - and not just during matches. Every team member must know what's expected of them and know what the current goals, tasks and strategies are.

5. **Constructive Conflict** - Discuss changes and resolve conflicts positively, and you'll save yourself a lot of upset. Keep the focus on choices and decisions - not on individuals.

6. **Cohesion** - You need to be a tight unit, and not just in-game - make sure you spend time together, just hanging out, either virtually or in real life.

7. **Credible Coaching** - If you want to use a coach, make sure you use someone who's actually a great coach, not just a great player - coaching is a skill in itself!

# Step 2: Apply the 7 Cs

Look at each of those 7 rules and work out how they apply to you as a team. What do you do well? What could you do better? If you can help create a team that hits all of these points, you'll be in very good shape indeed.

## The Do's and Don'ts of Being a Great Team Player

If you're still struggling to work out what you need to do to stay in everyone's good books, we've compiled a handy checklist for you:

### Living Together

- ✓ Keep communal areas clean.
- ✓ Create a cleaning rota - and stick to it!
- ✓ Pay your bills on time.
- ✗ Leave your dirty socks lying in the sink.

### Practicing Together

- ✓ Turn up to training events on time.
- ✓ Offer to help out others with any problems they're having.
- ✗ Rage quit every time you lose.

### Competing Together

- ✓ Follow instructions - even if you don't agree!
- ✓ Be kind and gracious in victory and in defeat.
- ✗ Blame the netcode if you lose.

### Hanging Together

- ✓ Make sure you socialise outside of just playing games together.
- ✓ Eat meals together - it's a great time to chat!
- ✗ Insist everyone listens to your Sqweee-Core Acid Step megamix at all times.

# COACH TRIP

## THINGS YOU WILL NEED ≫≫≫≫≫≫≫≫≫≫≫≫≫≫≫

SODA

PEN

PAD

When you're starting out, there's nothing wrong with asking for a helping hand. Just like with any sport, coaches can help you improve your game, push you harder, and teach you essential techniques.

## Step 1: Find a Coach

While there are some great coaching websites out there that will help match you with your perfect coach, you don't have to go splashing the cash right away. Other members of the gaming community or more experienced friends might be able to offer you some good advice when starting out for free.

### MATCHMAKING

If you do decide to go pro, try to use an organisation that has proper accreditation and good reviews. Don't be wowed by a list of famous or successful players they have on their books - the best players don't always make for the best teachers. Try to get a free trial session if you can, and see if you get along first.

## A Typical Coaching Session

Once you've found your coach, you'll need to start your training. This can be anything from once a week, to daily.

**PHASE 1**
**General Chat**
**Time:** 20 Mins
**Description:** A coaching session might start with a chat, where the coach will ask you what you've been doing well, and what you've been struggling with recently.

**PHASE 2**
**VOD Review**
**Time:** 1 Hour
**Description:** VOD stands for Video on Demand, but here it just means a video of one of your recent matches. The coach will take you through it, asking you questions, and pointing out where you could have done things better.

**PHASE 3**
**Drills**
**Time:** 2 Hours
**Description:** Drills are exercises that you'll perform, either solo or with your team. These will teach you certain plays, help you learn maps and build up your game knowledge.

**PHASE 4**
**Scrims**
**Time:** 2 Hours
**Description:** Scrims are practice matches. The aim is not so much to win, but to put the drills into practice and to improve communication as a team.

**PHASE 5**
**Homework**
**Time:** Various
**Description:** Yeah, you may not be in school, but there's always homework. The Coach will set you some tasks, including drills to practice, techniques to learn, or just a hefty helping of ranked play.

# INTERVIEW#3:
# THE
# ROOKIE

Remo 'Ray' Bügler is 28, and is just beginning his career in eSports. He's risen to the top of the pack on the European Hearthstone scene, and he attributes much of his success to using coaches from GamerSensei.com. We asked him how he got started, and how coaching had helped improve his game.

### HOW DID YOU FIRST GET INTERESTED IN ESPORTS?

REMO: My first eSports title was Warcraft 3, which I started playing when I was 12! For a long time I just played for fun, but eventually I got good enough to compete in the ESL "Alpen Amateur Series".

### WHAT WAS YOUR FIRST MAJOR COMPETITIVE EVENT LIKE?

REMO: My first major competition was online, when I was around 13 or 14, playing Warcraft 3. It was a decider match for entry to the ESL Pro Series. I was really nervous and I messed it up!

After this, I took a break, until I got involved with Hearthstone. Around two years ago, I started playing it competitively and had two great years. I won nearly every tournament I played in my country, got a good online ranking and then played for the Swiss National team at the Hearthstone Global Games in 2017. Now I'm trying something new, a game called Artifact.

### HAVE YOUR PARENTS BEEN SUPPORTIVE OF YOUR CAREER CHOICE?

REMO: Yes, my parents are still supporting me! My whole family, including my two brothers and my parents are also into gaming and eSports, so there was never any negative discussion about gaming - as long as we kept our school grades up!

### YOU USED COACHES EARLY ON, HOW DID THAT HELP?

REMO: I always wanted to get better, and at some point, you get tunnel vision and need help from outside to continue improving. A coach can help you see things you might miss, and will run drills to help you improve.

### WHAT SORT OF THINGS DID YOUR COACH HELP YOU WITH?

REMO: My coach worked on my individual needs and bad behaviours. Like in traditional sports training, you always have to go the extra mile and get out of your comfort zone. It's a lot of work and you need a lot of passion and stamina for what you're doing.

### WHAT'S YOUR TOP TIP FOR GETTING THE BEST OUT OF COACHING?

REMO: Be prepared and open minded. Whenever a coach is telling you something, try to listen, think about it and then discuss it with him. Communication is the key for success.

### DOES COACHING ALWAYS WORK?
REMO: Some people can improve without a coach. But they might be inconsistent and it's hard to unlearn bad behaviour. You can compare it to other sports like boxing: everyone can learn to box by themselves. But if you don't learn a technique correctly your jabs might not be effective enough and to later re-wire this behaviour is really hard.

### WHAT'S BEEN YOUR PROUDEST MOMENT IN ESPORTS?

REMO: Definitely the founding of my own eSports agency in 2018. It's called Epikk. I'm working on some really great projects, and it's amazing to be working on something that I love.

### WHAT DOES THE FUTURE HOLD FOR ESPORTS IN GENERAL?
REMO: Hard to say. It depends on what we do NOW, because we're creating the future and defining the way that eSports is going. No matter what, I'll be very excited to be a part of it!

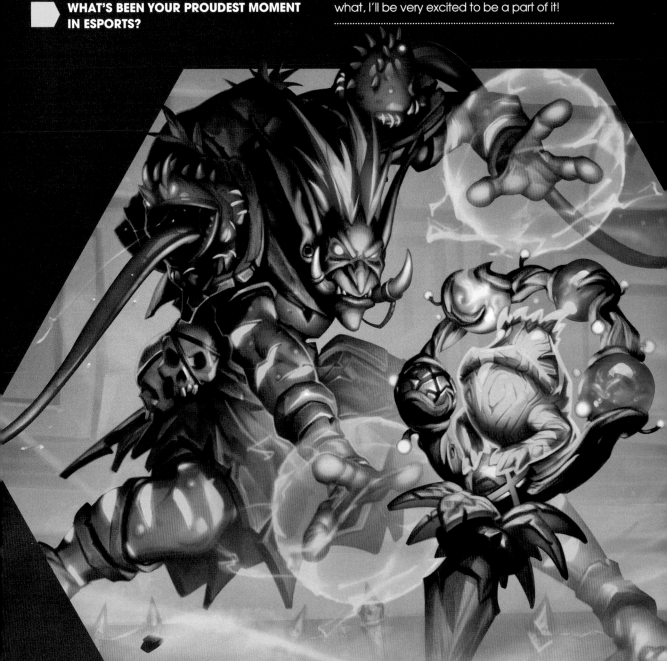

# YOUR FIRST COMP

## THINGS YOU WILL NEED ≫≫≫≫≫≫≫≫≫≫≫≫≫≫≫

**Your first competition can be a daunting experience. This is your first opportunity to show off what you can do. It may be a rude awakening!**

## Step 1: Finding a Tournament

Tournaments can be everything from a small local amateur event, all the way up to huge televised events - although this will probably be a long way off when you start. There are plenty of tournament providers like ESL, Gfinity and ELEAGUE, and they all offer amateur competitions where you can try your luck. Once you've gone through a registration process, it's usually just a case of picking your game and then searching for a tournament to enter.

## Step 2: Your First Match

Chances are you'll be a little nervous, so after you arrive, sign in and pick up any ID badges, make sure you find out exactly where you have to go, and when you have to be there. Then go and find a nice, quiet space and try to relax your mind.

**GAME ON**
When it's time for your match, remember that you want to do this as a career, so treat it as you would any other job - be friendly to your opponent, give the game 110%, and be gracious in both victory and defeat - after all, as much as you might want to rub your amazing victory in the

other player's face, sponsors may be watching! Whatever you do though, concentrate on achieving victory rather than showing off. Most matches will be in a 'Best of X' format, with X representing the maximum amount of games that will be played to determine a winner. This is usually shortened to BO1, BO2, etc.

## Step 3: Win the Tournament

Ok, this might be a little much on your first competition, but it certainly wouldn't hurt! If you can't manage that though, make sure you learn from the experience. What did you do well? What did you do badly? It's important to record these things, as you'll want to look back on these notes in the future.

# Tournament Types

Tournaments come in all shapes and sizes, but most of them will have either a single bracket or a double bracket elimination structure.

### SINGLE ELIMINATION BRACKET
Single Bracket is quite straightforward: The winner of each match will go forward until an eventual winner is declared:

**WINNER**

### DOUBLE ELIMINATION BRACKET
In a double elimination bracket tournament, the concept is the same, but the losers of the first set of matches get put into a lower bracket. The winner of the upper bracket and the winner of the lower bracket will ultimately face each other.

**Upper tier**

**WINNER**

**Lower tier**

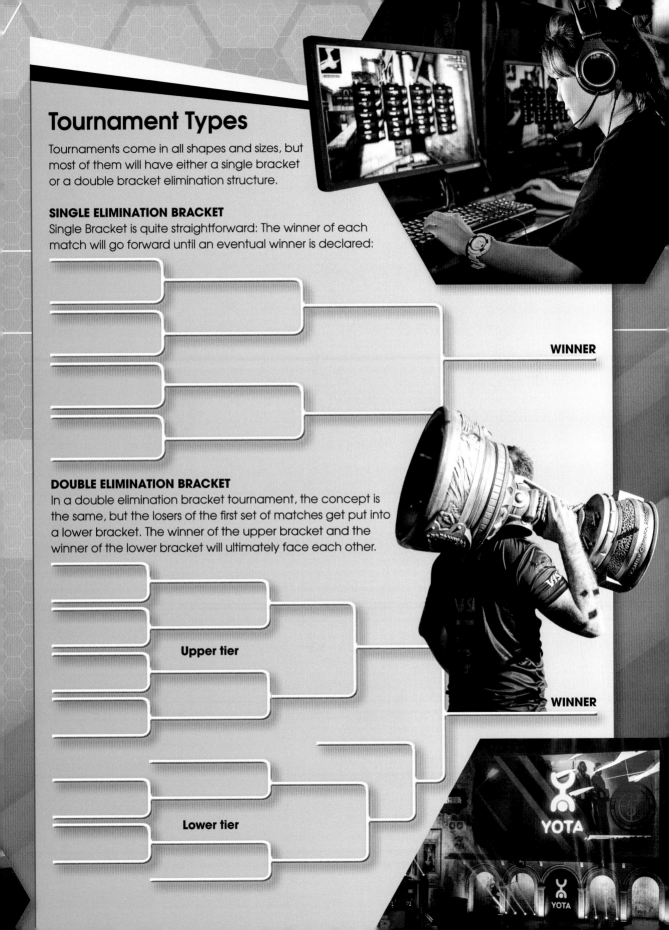

# LOSING WITH STYLE

Everyone wants to be a success. But learning how to deal with defeat is an important step on your journey. But how do you mentally prepare for potential failure?

## Step 1: Don't Punish Yourself

Sure, you might know exactly where you went wrong, the misplay that cost you the match. But don't start beating yourself up or obsessing over the one mistake you made. It's not healthy and you can't change it now anyway!

## Step 2: Take a Moment

When playing at a high level it can be easy to let the intensity get to you. So if you're playing a turn-based game, don't be afraid to take a little longer for your next move, or for action games, use the menu screens between matches to pause, reflect and re-centre yourself.

## Step 3: Learn From Your Mistakes

Make sure you review your VOD of the match after, and try to pinpoint where you went wrong - then adjust your training to iron out any blindspots you might have in your game.

## Step 4: Find Peace

Ok, so this set might not have gone your way. But look at everything else you've achieved. Enjoy the fact that you have a career you love. And shake your opponent's hand warmly, because although they won this round, they've also taught you everything you need to know about utterly destroying them the next time you meet.

# The Seven Stages of Losing a Match

This is what happens in your brain when you lose a match...

## 7 STAGES

| STAGE | EXPERIENCE | REACTION |
|---|---|---|
| Shock | The initial paralysis after losing the match | "What just happened?!" |
| Denial | Pretending it didn't happen | "No YOU just lost!" |
| Anger | Explosion of frustration | "Stupid keyboard!" |
| Bargaining | Attempting to find a way out | "Best of 5?" |
| Depression | The gloom descends | "Argh, I suck!" |
| Testing | Working out your next steps | "I need to practice more." |
| Acceptance | Finding a way forward | "It is what it is." |

# INTERVIEW#4:

# THE ANALYST

After a defeat, an analyst can really help you see where you went wrong. Jess Bolden is the Rainbow Six Siege analyst for the German eSports team PENTA Sports.

**SO JESS, WHAT DOES BEING AN ESPORTS ANALYST INVOLVE?**

JESS: Firstly, it involves finding numbers relevant to your opponents, whether it's preferred maps, operators or play styles. Then you need to be able to put this all down into numbers that can be made into tables and graphs/charts. This then all needs to be interpreted so you can best advise your team.

**WHICH IS THE MOST IMPORTANT SKILL FOR A GOOD ESPORTS ANALYST: NUMERICAL COMPETENCY, PSYCHOLOGICAL ASSESSMENT, OR THE ABILITY TO CONSUME VAST QUANTITIES OF ENERGY DRINKS?**

JESS: Most analysts agree that a coffee/energy drink is an absolute essential during work. As much as I would love to say that this is all it takes, being able to manipulate and aggregate numbers in different ways is vital. If it can be turned into numbers, you had better believe an analyst can do it.

**WHAT SORT OF QUALIFICATIONS DO YOU NEED TO BE A SUCCESSFUL ANALYST?**

JESS: There is not one single qualification one would need to get into this position. If you can prove that you can build an entire excel sheet with formulas and the information needed by the team, and then be able to interpret and explain it, then you're a good fit as an analyst.

**HOW DID YOU GET INVOLVED WITH PENTA?**

JESS: I was scrolling through Twitter and saw an advertisement by PENTA Sports for the Rainbow Six Siege analyst position. Next thing I knew I was undertaking a trial for them, against others, in order to prove my analytical abilities. The rest is history.

### HOW DID YOUR PARENTS REACT WHEN YOU TOLD THEM YOU WANTED TO WORK IN ESPORTS?

JESS: Before moving over to Europe to follow a career in eSports, I was teaching criminology and law in Melbourne, Australia. I think the big career shift was something they were surprised about. They did, however, know eSports was a big passion of mine and were super supportive of me following my passion.

### HOW DEEP IS YOUR KNOWLEDGE OF RAINBOW SIX SIEGE?

JESS: Having been a semi-professional, I had already put over 1500 hours into the game. I was, and am still, confident I can name any part of any map, or be able to utilise a high level of game sense in any situation. This is what it takes to be in the top tier of Rainbow Six Siege and it only gets more competitive every year.

### HOW DO ANALYSTS SEE GAMES DIFFERENTLY TO GAMERS?

JESS: I realised very quickly that once I had moved into a coaching/analyst role that I interpreted the game very differently to how I used to as a player. When you yourself are not in that stressful situation, you can calmly analyse the entire situation and better advise the team.

### IF YOU WANTED TO TAKE A MORE ANALYTICAL APPROACH TO YOUR GAMING, WHAT THINGS COULD YOU DO EASILY?

JESS: There are many behaviours gamers of all levels can adopt to improve their gaming. For example, in FPS games, learn how to aim head height and control any recoil. This often fixes the "I shot first but still died" phenomenon.

### WHAT'S BEEN YOUR BEST MOMENT WITH PENTA SO FAR?

JESS: I spent the first month with PENTA Sports living all the way in Melbourne, Australia. This meant I had to be up at all hours of the morning doing my coaching and analysing online and over the phone. So

I was half asleep at 4:00am during the Castle Siege competition, where with one eye open I watched as they became German champions. I felt so proud as they worked with me over the phone to make it happen.

### WHAT'S YOUR TOP TIP FOR GAMERS WHO WANT TO BECOME ANALYSTS?

JESS: Sometimes it means you may also need to coach, or work with other support staff. If you don't know how to put data into tables and charts, jump on YouTube and learn how to use Excel. My last bit of advice is to put yourself out there - find lower tier teams and volunteer as an analyst. Good luck!

# MONEY MAKIN'

The prize money at tournaments is increasing each year. In 2018, over $130 billion was given out in tournament prize money, almost $20 billion more than the year before. But it's not just winning tournaments that gets you income - you can also earn money from sponsors, coaching, Twitch and appearance fees.

## How Big Are The Tournament Prize Pots?

These can vary dramatically between tournaments. Some small regional tournaments will have small pots in the thousands, while world championship prize pots can be worth millions.

## How Does the Money Get Split?

The total prize pot will be split between winners, with the overall winners getting by far the biggest slice. This prize money will then generally get split between the team's organisers/management and the players themselves. Generally 10% of the winnings will go to the organisation, and then the rest will be divided amongst the players.

## What's a Yearly Income for a Pro Gamer?

As you'd expect, annual salaries can vary wildly depending on teams, ability and contracts. Top Dota 2 player Kuro Takhasomi has earned over $4 million in tournament money alone for example, while the vast majority of players will earn far, far less. Most pro gamers will be earning far more modest amounts though, somewhere between $1000 - $5000 a month.

## What If I'm Not in the Top 1% of Players?

There's no doubt that the earnings at the top can be great. But it's also important to bear in mind that the majority of eSports pros earn less than the minimum wage. You might have to learn how to live on very little in your first few years, and ultimately, if you don't think you'll be able to improve, you may have to decide if a career in eSports is for you. This is not necessarily unique to eSports - you don't have to look far to find stories of semi-pro football players who didn't quite make it to the big time.

## Piece of the Pie

Here's where the average pro gamer's income comes from.

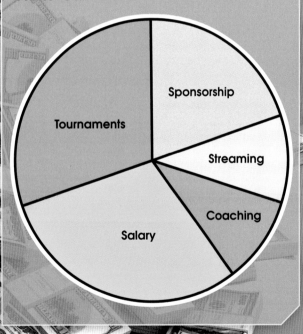

Sponsorship

Tournaments

Streaming

Coaching

Salary

# INTERVIEW#5:
# THE TOURNAMENT ORGANISERS

Since 2012, London-based Gfinity has made a name for itself as one of the biggest up-and-coming tournament organisers in the world. We asked Martin Wyatt, their Head of Publisher Relations, to talk about the tournament scene.

### ▶ IF SOMEONE WANTS TO GET INTO THE ESPORTS SCENE, WHAT ARE THE FIRST STEPS THEY SHOULD TAKE?

MARTIN:  Whether it's playing, casting, or working behind the scenes, you need to get to know the people involved, focus on an area you love and commit to it. The eSports community is tight-knit and always willing to offer advice so don't be afraid to speak to your peers to help you further your career.

*▶▶▶ Imagine organising all this - it's not easy, but it's fun!*

### ▶ HOW CAN GFINITY HELP YOUNG PLAYERS THAT ARE JUST GETTING INTO THE ESPORTS SCENE?

MARTIN: For players, the Challenger Series represents a realistic, fun, exciting way to take casual competitive gaming into a more professional direction. Through our online tournament we have discovered playing talent who have gone on to compete at elite level for world titles! Our biggest success story is Rannerz; he was drafted from the Challenger Series by AS Roma Fnatic and went on to win the FIFA 18 Elite Series.

### WHAT SHOULD A NOVICE PRO GAMER KNOW BEFORE THEY ENTER THEIR FIRST TOURNAMENT?

MARTIN: Be prepared to learn from the experience, be relaxed and just play to the best of your ability. Players need to play their own game and try not to do anything different. Also don't let the situation get the better of you. Try to play it like it's just another game.

### WHAT ARE THE INGREDIENTS OF A GREAT TOURNAMENT?

MARTIN: We are very lucky to have a league operations team that are experts in creating tournaments. First and foremost, they are core gamers and this is vital as they know what does and doesn't work. The tournaments must be credible in structure, and the formats should create exciting gameplay and unmissable content.

### HOW DOES GFINITY'S APPROACH TO ESPORTS DIFFER FROM OTHER TOURNAMENT ORGANISERS?

MARTIN: We care about two things more than any other: the games, and the people who play them. This focus keeps us very honest and able to produce tournaments and content that the community and the game publishers themselves are proud to be a part of. We also do everything in a bespoke fashion because we recognise that every community has their own identity and that needs to be celebrated.

### JUST AS IN ANY SPORT, HARASSMENT IN ESPORTS IS A MASSIVE ISSUE. HOW DO YOU POLICE ABUSIVE BEHAVIOUR DURING YOUR EVENTS?

MARTIN: We have always had a very robust approach to behaviour and conduct. Before any of our tournaments, players sign up to a strict code of conduct which outlines what is required of them behaviourally. We try to build relationships with all participants across the entire team so that everyone feels like they are driving the success of a tournament together.

### WHAT'S BEEN YOUR FAVOURITE TOURNAMENT MOMENT?

MARTIN: Toughest question ever! I think the one that stands out for me was at our first event, G1, in the Call of Duty: Black Ops II Semi Finals. We had Complexity facing off against the then world champions, Impact. It was incredibly close, aggressive, tense and had all the characteristics of a close competitive match.

### FINALLY, WHICH PLAYERS DO YOU THINK ARE GREAT AMBASSADORS FOR THE ESPORTS SCENE?

MARTIN: To single any one out is hard, however I think that people like Bruce Grannec, Raymond 'Rambo' Lussier, Jung 'MVP' Jong Hyun, Damon 'Karma' Barlow and Lee 'Faker' Sang-hyeok are all hall of fame names in their respective games that have gone on to inspire the next generation of players.

# SIGNAL BOOSTING

## THINGS YOU WILL NEED >>>>>>>>>>>>>>>>>>>>>>>>

CANDY

TWITTER ACCOUNT

FACEBOOK ACCOUNT

Now that you've got your team up and running, with hopefully a few victories under your belt, you're going to start telling people just how awesome you are. Yup, it's time to go viral!

## Step 1: Social Media

Twitter, Facebook and Instagram are great ways to let people know what's going on with your team. Twitter is best suited to short posts, Facebook pages are a great way to interact with fans, and Instagram is perfect for anything visual. Don't be afraid to be yourselves and show candid moments, bad times as well as good. Be professional though, and try not to get into flame wars!

## Step 2: Partner Up

Once you have a decent following, start pursuing partnerships. Big companies will send you free stuff for you to promote across your channels, but make sure it's a good fit for your brand first. When you do a promotion, don't try to make a professional advert - just tell your viewers why you like the product. If you can make it funny, then all the better.

## Step 3: Go Viral

Have you got a particularly funny bit of behind the scenes video, or a brilliant gaming goof? Upload it to your channel. If it seems to be getting a lot of likes and comments, you could even pay a bit extra to boost the post. Be creative!

## Step 4: Collaborate

Make friends with other teams, streamers and content makers. Do cross-channel collabs with them, and feed off each other's audiences. Appear on eSports podcasts. Become a yes person, and say 'yes' to any promotional opportunity you get in the first year of establishing yourself. Basically anything that you think will get your team's name out there, and establish you as fun, likable people.

# INTERVIEW#6:

# THE ESPORTS SUPERSTAR

One of the best Street Fighter players in the world, Daigo "The Beast" Umehara also holds the Guinness World Record for the largest amount of Street Fighter tournament wins. In 2017, he teamed up with Cygames to create Cygames Beast, an eSports team that aims to dominate the fighting games scene.

## WHY IS STREET FIGHTER SUCH A GOOD FIT FOR ESPORTS?

It has a lot to do with how widely known the game is. Many people are familiar with the characters and have a general idea of what kind of game it is. It's a fun game to play, of course, but also easy to understand what's going on at a glance, so it's also fun for spectators.

## WHAT IS YOUR TRAINING REGIME LIKE?

First thing after getting up in the morning, I do some tinkering with the game and investigate anything sticking in my mind from the night before. After eating breakfast, I go for a walk or head to the gym for some exercise. In the afternoon, I head out to train in offline matches. I'm out training until eleven at night, after which I go home and sleep.

## WHAT WAS IT THAT DREW YOU TO FIGHTING GAMES INITIALLY?

It may be hard to understand for modern gamers, but in those days, games featured small character sprites with minimal detail. Then Street Fighter 2 came along with its big, colourful characters - and they could talk!

## WHAT DROVE YOU TO BECOME SUCH A GREAT PLAYER?

In my teens, I was never much for just absorbing knowledge at face value without being able to apply it or see for myself. This took away my motivation, so of course I didn't fit in at school. I knew I wasn't a diligent kid, I was a screw-up, so I thought I'd never be able to surpass the bright and hardworking kids (at anything) unless I put in even more effort than them. So I found the one thing that I liked enough to put in the effort, so

that if it didn't work out, at least I could tell myself it was not my fault. I could think, "I gave it my all, so that's that." That was how I wanted to live.

I put so much effort into it in my teens it was like I was possessed, and people thought I was crazy. But my hard work back then has led to my current station in life.

## WHEN YOU STARTED PLAYING GAMES PROFESSIONALLY, WERE YOUR PARENTS AND TEACHERS SUPPORTIVE?

My parents supported my decision, but they told me that it probably wouldn't last forever so I should think about what I would do afterward.

There was no precedent for pro gamers in Japan. I was already an established figure within the industry and community, so there was this latent assumption or expectation that if anyone was going to go pro it'd be Umehara. When it happened, it was like, "Ah, Daigo finally went pro."

## IF SOMEONE WANTED TO DEDICATE THEMSELVES TO BECOMING A PROFESSIONAL GAMER, WHAT ADVICE WOULD YOU GIVE THEM?

Even if your wish comes true and you go pro, there's no guarantee you'll achieve success right away, and it's not always going to be this free-and-easy experience. For a while it'll be like you're feeling your way through a pitch-black tunnel. The key is in whether you have the courage and resolve to press forward anyway. Effort over talent. Effort is a pretence, and resolve a necessity. If you have the resolve to endure that hardship, then you should go for it.

### HOW MUCH TIME DO YOU PUT INTO LEARNING THE STREET FIGHTER GAMES' SECRETS?

There's no end to it. The more you know, the more you learn – it's an endless chain. So there's no magic number of hours or amount of effort that will make you a master of the game.

### JUST AS IN ANY SPORT, HARASSMENT IN ESPORTS IS AN ISSUE. HOW DO YOU KEEP COOL IF YOU GET ABUSE FROM FANS OR OTHER PLAYERS?

The culture within fighting games is such that you respect the opponent, even though there are instances of trash-talk. Sometimes the cheering in your opponent's corner will get too loud, but that's all part of fighting games. It's part of the eSports experience.

### DO YOU HAVE A SECRET ROUTINE TO PSYCHOLOGICALLY PREPARE YOURSELF BEFORE A MATCH?

For really important matches, I'll get some time on the game beforehand and do some light warm-up exercises. There's a link between your physical condition and your mental wherewithal.

### HOW DOES IT FEEL WHEN YOU STEP OUT ON STAGE WITH THOUSANDS OF PEOPLE CHANTING YOUR NAME?

It's not something that brings me joy or amusement, per se; rather, there's a strong feeling of gratitude. Before becoming a pro gamer, I'd only had sporadic employment, and this was my only special skill. I wouldn't exist as a pro gamer without the fans, so my gratitude is unfading.

### WHICH WIN FROM YOUR CAREER WAS THE MOST SATISFYING, AND WHY?

My win at the Alpha 3 National Tournament. That and my 2009 EVO win, which marked my return after a several-year hiatus. Those made me happy, pure and simple. They were the catalysts for my becoming a pro. If those wins hadn't happened, I'd be living a different life.

### IF YOU SUFFER A DEFEAT, HOW DO YOU CHEER YOURSELF UP?

I just have to keep going. I have to move on. I can't afford to get hung up.
The pro-tour is a year-around venture, and after the current season ends, a new season starts. My competitor life doesn't stop after one tournament.

### HOW HAS THE FORMATION OF THE CYGAMES BEAST TEAM HELPED YOUR CAREER? WHAT SUPPORT HAVE THEY GIVEN YOU?

Fighting games are a one-on-one activity, so I've always fought alone, but with the formation of this team there's a new feeling of solidarity (though the game itself remains 1v1), and I enjoy that.

### If you could pick one opponent to face in the ultimate Street Fighter V bout, who would you pick and why?

The lineup of players composing the top echelon is in constant flux, so I personally find it hard to settle on one rival. It's more like I'm the constant factor and everything around me is always changing. So I only focus on self-improvement, getting stronger today than I was yesterday.

# FIND A
# SPONSOR

## THINGS YOU WILL NEED »»»»»»»»»»»»»»»»»

While you can earn money from social media, coaching and winning tournaments, if you're going to survive as a team, you'll ultimately need a good sponsor. So how do you actually get one?

BRIEFCASE

CALCULATOR

SANDWICHES

## Step 1: What Sort of Sponsorship Are You Looking For?

Firstly, you have to decide what sort of sponsorship you're looking for. The main types are:

| | |
|---|---|
| **INFORMAL SPONSORS** | These guys will offer you small, one off deals in exchange for promoting their brands across your channels. |
| **TECHNICAL SPONSORS** | They will offer equipment or services in exchange for promotion, a very common arrangement in eSports circles. |
| **OFFICIAL SPONSORS** | They'll offer a larger amount of money, usually aimed at a certain goal, like accommodation. |
| **GENERAL SPONSOR** | These guys will want their brand plastered all over your channels and clothing. In exchange, they'll provide a large chunk of your funding. |
| **TITLE SPONSOR** | This is the full ride. These sponsors will take care of almost everything for you. All you have to do is keep winning... |

# Step 2: Making Your Approach

Most brands associated with eSports will have a set of guidelines on their website - make sure you read these carefully, and that you tick all the boxes. Once you're sure that you do, plan your opening gambit carefully. Don't just tweet badly composed @ messages to them - find their contact email address, and compose a short email, detailing why you think your team would be a good fit for them, what you think you can offer, and ask how you can progress your application. Remember, politeness never hurts! Don't be disheartened if a response takes a while - large companies tend to move very slowly.

# Step 3: The Art of the Deal

Once you've got a sponsor interested, you'll need to agree on a deal. It's a good idea to talk to other teams at your level about their deals, so you can get a good idea of what you should be asking for. It's important to know your worth, or you could leave money on the table. Also make sure you read any contracts, and get a parent or ideally a lawyer to look at it before you sign anything - or you may regret it later. Finally, if a deal doesn't feel right to you, don't be afraid to walk away. There will be other opportunities!

# What Are Sponsors Looking For?

Most sponsors are looking at three things. If you can be in the middle of this Venn diagram, then you're in good shape.

**TEAM**
Who's in the team and why are they unique?

**AUDIENCE**
How much of a following do you have?

**COST**
What are you asking for?

# GLOBAL OFFENSIVE

## THINGS YOU WILL NEED »»»»»»»»»»»»»»»

Once your team is sponsored, it's time to travel the world! Top pro gamers will travel over 40 times a year to competitions. Here's where you'll go, when you go pro.

**PASSPORT**

**TRAVEL PILLOW**

**NINTENDO SWITCH**

## Vancouver, Canada

**DOTA 2: THE INTERNATIONAL**
Grab yourself some poutine and a seat with some of the best Dota 2 players in the world.

## Las Vegas, USA

**EVO CHAMPION SERIES**
This annual competition sees the best fighting games experts clash in the dry heat of this gambling mecca. Shoryuken!

## California, USA

**OVERWATCH WORLD CUP FINALS**
Taking place at the annual BlizzCon event, this is one of the glitziest events around. You'll also be able to take in Hearthstone and StarCraft II competitions too!

## Paris, France

### PARIS GAMES WEEK
This event often features large eSports events, featuring games like Hearthstone and Clash Royale. Ooh la la!

## London, UK

### F1 ESPORTS PRO SERIES
If you're a petrolhead, you'll be heading to London for the tournament that's driving everyone crazy - just don't forget your leather gloves.

## Monaco, France

### FIA GT CHAMPIONSHIP
The finals for the biggest event on the Gran Turismo racing calendar, you'll be heading to the beautiful French Riviera to fight it out for pole position.

## Tokyo, Japan

### CRL WORLD FINALS
Here you'll be playing against the best Clash Royale players in the world.

## Seoul, South Korea

### LEAGUE OF LEGENDS WORLD CHAMPIONSHIPS
If you're a LoL player, you'll have to go to South Korea to really prove your worth. The 2018 competition had a peak viewership of 200 million viewers!

## Katowice, Poland

### IEM CS: GO WORLD CHAMPIONSHIPS
Taking place in sunny Katowice, the Counter Strike: Global Operations World Championships are a highlight of the eSports calendar.

# I KNOW YA GOT SEOUL!

When it comes to competitive gaming, there's nowhere quite like South Korea. It's like a window into the future, showing how big eSports could be in the West in 10 years time. Start practicing your Korean now!

## The History

South Korea was slow to adopt console gaming, and in the early 90s, a rash of reports inspired the government to introduce legislation that effectively killed the spread of console culture. As a result, the PC flourished there, and coupled with the explosion in popularity of internet cafés in the early 90s, online gaming became popular there long before it spread to the rest of the world. Games like Lineage, Nexus and Maple Story took off in a big way, and their success inspired Western games like World of Warcraft.

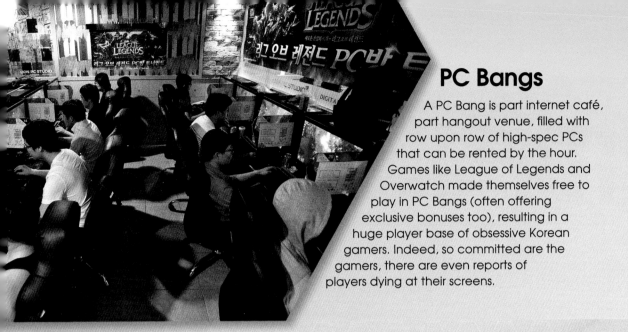

## PC Bangs

A PC Bang is part internet café, part hangout venue, filled with row upon row of high-spec PCs that can be rented by the hour. Games like League of Legends and Overwatch made themselves free to play in PC Bangs (often offering exclusive bonuses too), resulting in a huge player base of obsessive Korean gamers. Indeed, so committed are the gamers, there are even reports of players dying at their screens.

## The Tournaments

South Korea created the World Cyber Games in 2000, and in 2005 the Yongsan ESports Stadium was built, the first of its kind anywhere in the world. Events are broadcast to millions of viewers, the pro sports players are on six-figure contracts, and they're treated like genuine celebrities.

## Asian Games 2018

The 2018 Asian Games even included eSports as a category. The games played included StarCraft II, League of Legends, and Hearthstone. South Korea managed to place joint second with Indonesia, whilst first place was taken by China.

# FAN MAIL

## THINGS YOU WILL NEED >>>>>>>>>>>>>>>>>>>>>

SHARPIE

PAIN KILLERS

TEA

Once you do make it big, you'll have to deal with fans. That might sound awesome - and it can be! But not all interactions will be positive. Here's a few steps you can take to navigate these difficult waters.

## Step 1: Be Kind and Patient

Yes, you might be exhausted. No, you might not want to talk to this person right now. But a positive interaction with a fan will be something they remember for years. It doesn't matter if you're tired, or you've just lost a match, or lost a sponsorship deal - putting on a grin for a selfie is the least you can do.

## Step 2: Put Yourself in Their Shoes

Think about people that you're fanatical about. Imagine how you'd feel if you met them. Awestruck, maybe? Afraid you might say something dumb or even upset them? Meeting your idols is tough, and this is what's going through the mind of your fans when they nervously meet you. So if they do say something dumb, just laugh it off, or ignore it.

## Step 3: Be the Bigger Person

Sometimes you'll come across someone who's spoiling for a fight. They might be flaming you online or even being aggressive in person. Do not engage if you can avoid it - remember, words live on the internet forever, everyone has a smartphone, and even if it would feel so good to put them on blast, it'll be much better for future you if you just go and write something nasty about them in your private journal instead.

## Step 4: Protect Yourself

Sadly, in this day and age, things like swatting (people calling the police on you while you're streaming) and doxxing (people digging out your personal details and posting them on the web) are real things. So protect yourself as much as possible. Never give out your real address, turn off geotagging on your social posts, and don't put any important personal details online.

## Step 5: Stay Frosty

There will always be opportunists attracted to success and fame, and although it won't always be easy to separate those who are genuine and those who are not, do be careful about who you let into your life - especially if they seem more interested in the trappings of your fame than you as a person.

# WINNER, WINNER!

So you made it. You travelled the world and you won every tournament going. Well, success is great, but what comes next? Here are a few suggestions on post-pro gaming careers.

## Shoutcasting

**AVERAGE SALARY:** Around $1000/day

If you have the gift of the gab, shoutcasting can be a great career. You'll be able explain what's going on in the player's heads, because you've been there. Panel Analysts usually provide the pre-and post match chat in the studio, Play-by-Play commentators discuss the match while it's in progress, and Hosts introduce the show and interview the competitors.

## Coaching

**AVERAGE SALARY:** $40k/year

Coaching is not just about being good at a game - it's about using technique and psychology to help other players break through walls and improve their game. It can be incredibly rewarding though, and there's no feeling quite like seeing one of your students taking everything you've taught them and using it to win.

# Consulting

**AVERAGE SALARY:**
Around $1000/day

This job sees you playing games in development, and helping the developers tweak the experience so that it plays just right. This a great role if you like to analyse games and try to work out what's going on under the bonnet.

# Community Management

**AVERAGE SALARY:** Around $35k/year

If you enjoy the social media aspect of eSports, this could be a great role for you. You'll mainly be chatting to fans online, creating content and acting as a conduit between the fans and the developers. You'll definitely need a cool head and a calm demeanour though, as not every interaction you have with fans will be positive!

# Player Management

**AVERAGE SALARY:**
Around $80k/year

Player management is all about the art of the deal, so if you have a particularly good head for business and socialising, this could be the role for you. Be warned though, the hours are long, there's lots of travel and you'll not have much time to play games anymore. But the rewards are certainly worth it!

# THE TOP 20 ESPORTS TITLES YOU MUST PLAY

There are hundreds of games out there that can be played as an esport, but only a handful attract huge audiences and large paychecks. But it can be difficult to pick a game to specialise in. To get you started, we've picked 20 of the most interesting and important eSports titles on the scene for you to try out.

# FORTNITE

Fortnite's Battle Royale free-to-play multiplayer mode has taken the gaming world by storm, offering epic battles with a hefty side-order of goofy humour. By the end of 2018, the game had reached a massive monthly player base of over 78m players.

Year of release: **2017**
Developer: **Epic Games**
eSports platform: **PC/PS4/Xbox One/iOS/Android**
Team or solo play: **Both**
Average match length: **20-25m**
Play method: **Keyboard and mouse/gamepad**
Accessibility: ★★★★

## Trivia

On March 15th, 2018, famous Twitcher Tyler "Ninja" Blevins broke the internet with his Fortnite stream that also featured rapper Drake. At its peak, their joint Twitch stream featured over 635,000 concurrent viewers, smashing the previous records by hundreds of thousands of viewers.

# 'Nite Fever

One of the newest games on the eSports scene, Fortnite is still in its infancy as an eSport, and leagues are still being established. Epic have a lot of faith in the game's prospects, and they've pumped over $100m into its eSports fund, including the Fortnite World Cup, open to both solo players and duos. This is a great opportunity to get in at the ground floor at what is sure to be one of the biggest eSports games around.

## How to Play

Fortnite is a 100 player vs. player Battle Royale, which sees you fighting against everyone else on a single map, until only one player is left. The map is updated and changed every season. But you knew all that!

- Each match starts on the flying battle bus as it flies over the map, ejecting players as it goes. Once you've jumped, you can glide your character down to the ground.

- Once landed, you must quickly gather resources and weapons - hopefully before anyone else can take you out!

- After a few minutes, a storm will slowly encroach onto the map, pushing all the players inside a large circular area.

- Circles will continue to appear on the map, each one making the playing area even smaller, increasing the chance of a confrontation with other players.

- Players can go on the offensive, build structures to defend themselves, or even hide completely!

## Top Competition

**Name:** Fortnite Winter Royale ● **Location:** Online ● **Prize Pool:** $1m
**Description:** Fortnite is still relatively young in eSports, so the Fortnite Winter Royale event in 2018 was Epic's first major tournament, with a prize pool of $1m. Acting as a test run for 2019's first Fortnite World Cup, the tournament was open to all players.

# LEAGUE OF LEGENDS

League of Legends is one of the biggest eSports titles in the world. It was one of the first eSports to be featured in the Asian Games, in 2018, and has over 100 million active players every month.

Year of release: **2009**

Developer: **Riot Games**

eSports platform: **PC/Mac OS**

Team or solo play: **Team**

Average match length: **30m - 1hr**

Play method: Keyboard and Mouse

Accessibility: ★★★★★

## The League's League

League of Legends has an extremely active eSports community and top players compete in Riot Games' League of Legends Championships Series, which culminates in the annual League of Legends World Championship tournament.

## Easy to Start, Hard to Master

With over 140 characters to master, the game can be quite daunting at first, but it features excellent tutorials, and a requirement to master the game up to Level 30 before you can participate in ranked matches, giving you plenty of time to practice before things get real. Because of this, it's considered one of the most accessible eSports around.

# How to Play

League of Legends is a MOBA (Massively Online Battle Arena) game. Although there are 3 different maps, Summoner's Rift is the most popular.

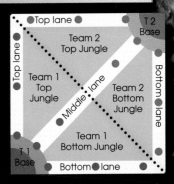

Each team has a Nexus in their base that they must defend from the other team.

The Nexus spawns minions, which will march down one of three 'lanes' towards the other player's base.

Lanes contain towers and inhibitors. You'll need to destroy these before you can hurt the other player's Nexus.

Player characters are not restricted to the lanes, and can roam anywhere on the map. It's their job to destroy enemy minions and towers, protect friendly minions and towers, as well as complete other objectives along the way.

Other tasks include destroying jungle monsters, elemental drakes and Elder Dragons.

Completing these objectives earns buffs and gold, which you can use to purchase items and abilities. Destroy the enemy's Nexus to win!

# Top Competition

**Name:** League of Legends World Championship ● **Location:** Paris (2019)
**Prize Pool:** $2m+ ● **Description:** One of the glitziest events in the eSports calendar, the League of Legends World Championship is a globe trotting event that switches location each year. The 2018 event was held in South Korea - in 2019 it'll be held in Paris, France. It's incredibly popular - in 2017, the finals were watched by over 60 million viewers worldwide.

# STREET FIGHTER V

This series has always been at the forefront of the competitive gaming scene, firstly in the arcades, then the living room and now online. Launched in 2016, Street Fighter V has been specifically designed with tournament play in mind.

Year of release: **2016**
Developer: **Capcom/Dimps**
eSports platform: **Xbox One/ PS4/PC**
Team or solo play: **Solo**
Average match length: **2-4 mins**
Play method: **Gamepad/ Fight Stick**
Accessibility: ★★

## Trivia

In Street Fighter V, Chun Li's Critical Art has 37 hits. This is a reference to the legendary fight at Evo 2004, when Street Fighter god Daigo Umehara perfectly parried Justin Wong's Chun Li Super Art in a Street Fighter III: 3rd Strike bout. Look for it on YouTube under the title 'Evo Moment #37' - it has over 2.7 million views to date.

## Sonic Boom!

At a pro level, Street Fighter is an insanely technical game, and you'll be competing against some players who have almost 30 years of muscle memory flowing through their veins. You'll also need to master the arcade-style fight stick, as no self-respecting Street Fighter player would be seen dead near a game pad. But if you can put the time in, and train as hard as Ryu, then maybe, just maybe, you'll be able to play on an international level. That may sound daunting, but as Lao Tzu once said: "The journey of one thousand miles begins with a single Hadouken."

# How to Play

1. 
2. 
3. 
4. 
5. 
6. 
7. 

1. **Health Gauge** - This is how much health your character currently has. If it gets to zero, you lose the round.

2. **Stun Gauge** - This increases the more hits you take - if it fills up completely, your character will become stunned and vulnerable to punishment from the other player.

3. **Time** - This is how long the round has left. If the time runs out, the player with the highest remaining health will win.

4. **Win Mark** - This shows how many rounds your player has won.

5. **Character** - This is your current character.

6. **V-Gauge** - This gauge fills up as you take hits from your opponent. As blocks fill, you can spend them on V-Triggers and V-Reversals.

7. **Critical Gauge** - Land blows to fill this meter, and when full, unleash your earth-shaking Critical Art. Unlike V-Gauge, this carries over between rounds.

# Top Competition

**Name:** Evo Championship Series ● **Location:** Mandalay Bay, Las Vegas
**Prize Pool:** $84,000 ● **Description:** Evo is the biggest event on the fighting tournament calendar. Founded by Tom Cannon in 1996, it has moved from its humble origins in California to a glitzy annual event in Las Vegas. Although many different fighting games are played there, the Street Fighter series has always been a permanent fixture, and it's where all the top players go to test their mettle. When it comes to Street Fighter, this is where you earn your belts.

# FIFA 19

With a new game out every year since 1993, FIFA has mostly ruled the footy roost for the last 25 years. In the last few years, the series has gone from strength to strength, becoming the best-selling sports franchise in the world, with over 260 million copies sold.

Year of release: **2018**

Developer: **EA**

eSports platform: **PC/PS4/ Xbox One**

Team or solo play: **Solo**

Average match length: **12-14 minutes**

Play method: **Gamepad**

Accessibility: ★★★

## E we go, e we go, e we go!

FIFA is a huge eSports success story, with EA running an annual World Cup series since 2004. The FIFA 18 Ultimate Team (FUT) mode (first introduced way back in FIFA 09) is now a cornerstone of the FIFA experience, and FUT players compete annually to lead their squads on the path to victory. Events are televised, streamed and dissected by casters who offer play-by-plays on all the big matches. Competition is fierce though, so if you want to win, you're going to have to eat, sleep and dream FIFA.

## Trivia

For the epic reveal trailer for FIFA 19, EA enlisted the help of famed movie composer Hans Zimmer to adapt the UEFA Champions League anthem, with the help of rapper Vince Staples. Zimmer took the job seriously, saying that with something this big you have to "be bold, be brave. Go big or, truly, stay home". Here's hoping EA will get him to have a crack at the similarly epic Ski Sunday theme next.

# How to Play

FIFA 19's basic rules are the same as any other football match - you have 90 minutes (sped up to 6 minutes/half) to score more goals than the other team.

### BEST ATTACKING FORMATION

Just like in real football, the 4-2-3-1 formation dominates FIFA, and it's easy to see why. It can easily absorb pressure from the other side, and it's always ready to flip into an attacking position. You'll want two fast dribblers on the left and right midfield, and a creative passer in the central position, someone who's always ready to place the ball at the feet of the solitary striker.

Striker

Left Midfield

Right Midfield

Attacking Midfielder

Defensive Midfielder

Defensive Midfielder

Left Back

Centre Back

Centre Back

Right Back

### BEST WAY TO SCORE GOALS

In FIFA 19, the new Low Shot will help you score more goals than Ronaldo. Firstly, get near the box with a clear shot on goal. Slow your pace to draw the goalie out, then hold L1 + R1, and hold the shoot button just a fraction longer than necessary to charge your shot. You'll bury the shot in the back of the net almost every time.

# Top Competition

**Name:** The FIFA eWorld Cup
**Location:** Various
**Prize Pool:** $400,000
**Description:** The eWorld Cup has been run since 2004, but things didn't get serious until 2016, when the prize money and media attention started to leap up exponentially. In 2018, the winner was Mossad 'Msdossary' Aldossary who won $250,000 after giving 'StefanoPinna' a thorough 4:0 kicking in the Grand Final at The O2 in London.

# OVERWATCH

Rising like a phoenix from the ashes of Blizzard's cancelled Titan project, Overwatch is nothing short of a phenomenon. With a player base of over 40 million players, its success can be attributed to its bold, colourful aesthetic, the larger than life hero characters, and the rich, detailed setting.

Year of release: **2017**

Developer: **Polyphony Digital**

eSports platform: **PS4**

Team or solo play: **Solo**

Average match length: **10 mins**

Play method: **Steering Wheel/Gamepad**

Accessibility: ★★★★

## It Came in Like a Wrecking Ball

Although not originally designed with eSports in mind, Overwatch has become a huge game on the pro circuit. Overwatch is a particularly good choice for new players wanting to dip their toes into eSports. The rules are easy to learn, there's enough characters to experiment with, but not so many that the choice is daunting, and the community is generally noted for being friendly. There's also a well-presented ranking system, which helps players stand out when pro teams come scouting for new talent.

## Trivia

Doomfist was a character name originally thrown out jokingly in an early brainstorming session for the game, but a sketch of the character captured the fans imaginations, and he was eventually added to the roster of characters. Brooklyn 99 actor (and avid gamer) Terry Crews offered to voice the character for Blizzard, but sadly nothing came of it.

King's Row 629

OFFENSE

DEFENSE

▲ TANK

SELECTED

# Class is in Session

If you're going to learn how to dominate the maps, you're going to have to learn the classes in Overwatch. Here's a handy guide to the three main classes: Damage, Tank and Support.

**DAMAGE CLASS**
**Team role:** Throw out as much firepower as quickly as possible, either offensively or defensively.
**Best suited to:** Lone wolf players that like to show off.
**Example characters:** Soldier 76, Genji, Pharah
**Get good at:** Pharah - her flight abilities can get you out of trouble quickly, her rockets lay down some good damage, and frankly she's just cool as hell.

**TANK CLASS**
**Team role:** Soak up damage from the opposing team, and cause distractions.
**Best suited to:** Chaos worshippers
**Example characters:** D. Va, Roadhog, Winston
**Get good at:** Winston - his shield will save your team time and time again, and his ability to perform a leaping smash into enemies is always fun.

**SUPPORT CLASS**
**Team role:** Healing and buffing your team-mates.
**Best suited to:** Motherly figures.
**Example characters:** Mercy, Symmetra, Zenyatta
**Get good at:** Mercy - Mercy's heavenly healing abilities include the ability to raise team-mates from the dead, and an ultimate that when used appropriately can turn the tide of a match. What an angel!

# Top Competition

**Name:** Overwatch World Cup ● **Location:** BlizzCon, Anaheim, California **Prize Pool:** $488,000 ●
**Description:** The final of the Overwatch World Cup is held every year at BlizzCon, the annual celebration of all things Blizzard. For the last few years the competition has been dominated by the South Korean team, who won again in 2018.

# GRAN TURISMO SPORT

The ultimate racing series for petrolheads, few other racing games come close to matching Gran Turismo's level of detail. So influential are the Gran Turismo games, Nissan actually reported a huge uptick in Skyline sales after the car's inclusion in the first game!

Year of release: **2017**

Developer: **Polyphony Digital**

eSports platform: **PS4**

Team or solo play: **Solo**

Average match length: **10 mins**

Play method: **Steering Wheel/Gamepad**

Accessibility: ★★★★

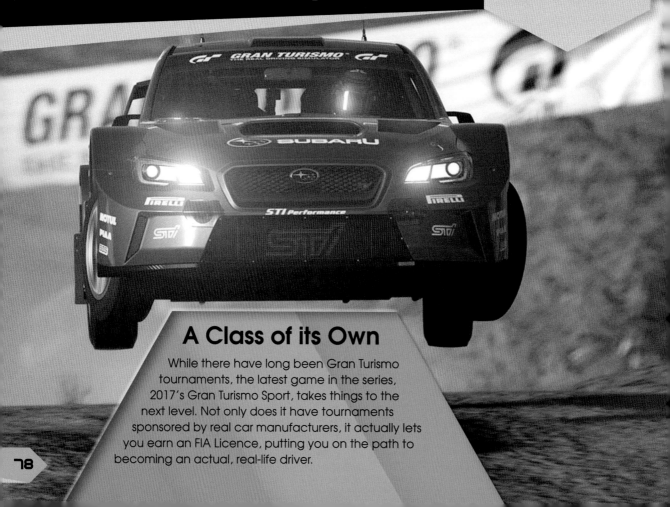

## A Class of its Own

While there have long been Gran Turismo tournaments, the latest game in the series, 2017's Gran Turismo Sport, takes things to the next level. Not only does it have tournaments sponsored by real car manufacturers, it actually lets you earn an FIA Licence, putting you on the path to becoming an actual, real-life driver.

## Trivia

Like Ernest Hemingway and Orson Welles before him, Kazunori Yamauchi has a street named after him in Rondo, Spain. Announced by the mayor when Yamauchi chose the small city for the launch event for Gran Turismo 6, the road apparently offers some wonderful views of the famous Puente Nuevo bridge.

## Track Mania

When racing, it's important to know your tracks. Here's a guide to classic racing track Brands Hatch to get you started.

1. **Paddock Hill Bend -** It's hard to see the apex on this turn, start braking as soon as you pass the marshall's post.

2. **Druids Bend -** A tight hairpin. Brake on the walkway, and try to keep a tight corner, before accelerating out.

3. **Hawthorn Bend -** A deceptively simple corner, the trick is to maintain a constant speed.

4. **Westfield Bend -** The shortest driving line is across the inner kerbstone - make sure you use your throttle to keep your car stable.

5. **Sheene's Curve -** The exit here has a narrow width, so set your apex slightly later than you would normally.

6. **Stirling's Bend -** An almost 90 degree corner that allows for a high speed turn.

7. **Clark Curve -** A tricky corner, it's imperative you get your racing line right here.

### Brands Hatch

## Top Competition

**Name:** FIA GT Championship ● **Location:** Monaco ● **Prize Pool:** FIA GT Championship Trophy, racing contract. ● **Description:** Taking place in Monaco on the French Riviera, the FIA GT Championship has a spectacular location for it's World Final. Winners from the regional finals gather here to race for the ultimate prize - a real-life racing contract, and the chance to be crowned world champion on the same stage that F1 drivers collect their champagne.

# ROCKET LEAGUE

Rocket League was a huge success right out of the gate, and it's only grown in popularity. Part of its success can be attributed to the simplicity of its concept - football, but with rocket powered vehicles!

Year of release: **2015**
Developer: **Psyonyx**
eSports platform: **PC/Mac OS/ Xbox One/PS4/Switch**
Team or solo play: **Team**
Average match length: **5 mins**
Play method: **Gamepad**
Accessibility: ★★★

## Chevy Metal

Much of Rocket League's early success was thanks to gamers watching spectacular highlights reels on social media. Although straightforward to pick up initially, Rocket League can be very demanding technically, and you'll need to work well as part of a team if you're serious about becoming a Rocket League champion.

# Skin Game

One of the best things about Rocket League are the vehicle skins that Psyonyx make available to the players as DLC. Here's some of our favourites.

**Vehicle:** DeLorean Time Machine
**Body Type:** Octane
**Inspired by:** Back to the Future Part II (1989)
**Why we love it:** Well, if you're gonna play Rocket League, why not do it with some style? The attention to detail is just awesome - fly too high, and the wheels fold in, just like in the movie. Plus, if you get destroyed, the car disappears in a flash, leaving two trails of fire and a spinning 'OUTTATIME' number plate. Heavy!

**Vehicle:** '89 Batmobile
**Body Type:** Dominus
**Inspired by:** Batman (1989)
**Why we love it:** You'd have to be a Joker not to want one of these sweet babies. Jets of fire shoot out the back, as you show off your skills and represent for Gotham in the League. Just don't ask for an interview with the driver post-match - he's bats.

**Vehicle:** Jeep Wrangler
**Body Type:** Octane
**Inspired by:** Jurassic Park (1993)
**Why we love it:** Found in the DNA of a Jeep encased in amber, this vehicle is no dinosaur. Crank up the John Williams and watch out for the incredible flaming T-Rex goal explosion!

## Trivia

Rocket League has been a great success, but a lot of that is thanks to lessons learned from the production of (deep breath) 'Supersonic Acrobatic Rocket-Powered Battle-Cars', Psyonix's first attempt at a car-based football game. Released on PS3 to little fanfare in 2008, it didn't help that, according to Rocket League designer Corey Davis it had "the worst game name of all time."

## Top Competition

**Name:** Rocket League Championship Series
**Location:** Various ● **Prize Pool:** $1m
**Description:** The Rocket League Championship Series is run by Psyonix twice a year, with the finals held in a different location each time. The prize money has been creeping up each year, hitting $1m for the first time in 2018. In 2017, Psyonix added a second lower league, the Rocket League Rivals Series, with teams being promoted and relegated between the leagues at the end of each season.

# SUPER SMASH BROS. ULTIMATE

| | |
|---|---|
| Year of release: | **2018** |
| Developer: | **Bandai Namco Studios** |
| eSports platform: | **Switch** |
| Team or solo play: | **Both** |
| Average match length: | **5 mins** |
| Play method: | **Gamepad** |
| Accessibility: | ★★★ |

Super Smash Bros. is a game series that started out decades before eSports were taken seriously, that has subsequently become one of the most popular games on the fighting tournament scene. Much of Super Smash Bros. Ultimate's success can be attributed to its fast play style, its loving attention to detail and the sheer fun of finding out who would win in a fight between Solid Snake and Pikachu!*

## Trivia

Although beloved game director Masahiro Sakurai is perhaps best known for his work on the Super Smash Bros. series, he also created everyone's favourite whimsical candy floss blowhard Kirby, when he was just 19 years old.

## Let's a Go!

Usually played as either singles or doubles matches, Smash tournaments have strict rules. Matches are played in best-of-three sets, items are turned off, timers are set, and each player has a set number of lives (aka "stocks"). At its highest level the competition is extremely fierce, and with the exception of Swedish players William Peter Hjelte and Adam Lindgren, it's largely dominated by US players, a rarity in the pro-fighting tournament scene.

*In case you were wondering, it's Pikachu.*

# How to Play

Super Smash Bros. varies between titles, but the essentials always remain the same: Get your opponent's smash percentage as high as possible, and then perform a smash attack to knock them out of the arena.

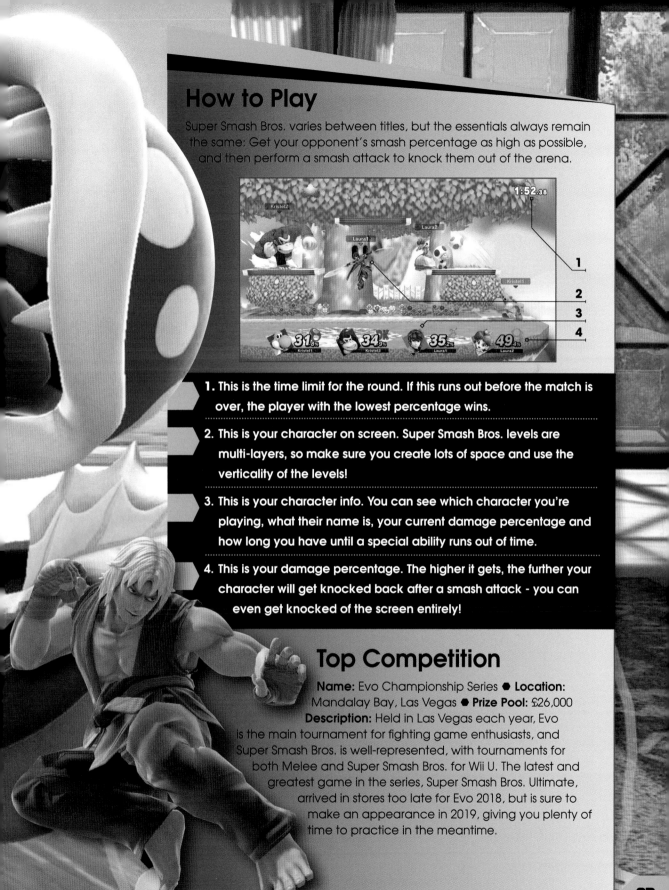

**1.** This is the time limit for the round. If this runs out before the match is over, the player with the lowest percentage wins.

**2.** This is your character on screen. Super Smash Bros. levels are multi-layers, so make sure you create lots of space and use the verticality of the levels!

**3.** This is your character info. You can see which character you're playing, what their name is, your current damage percentage and how long you have until a special ability runs out of time.

**4.** This is your damage percentage. The higher it gets, the further your character will get knocked back after a smash attack - you can even get knocked of the screen entirely!

## Top Competition

**Name:** Evo Championship Series ● **Location:** Mandalay Bay, Las Vegas ● **Prize Pool:** £26,000
**Description:** Held in Las Vegas each year, Evo is the main tournament for fighting game enthusiasts, and Super Smash Bros. is well-represented, with tournaments for both Melee and Super Smash Bros. for Wii U. The latest and greatest game in the series, Super Smash Bros. Ultimate, arrived in stores too late for Evo 2018, but is sure to make an appearance in 2019, giving you plenty of time to practice in the meantime.

# CALL OF DUTY: BLACK OPS IIII

Year of release: **2018**

Developer: **Activision**

eSports platform: **PC/Xbox One/PS4**

Team or solo play: **Team**

Average match length: **25 -30 mins**

Play method: **Keyboard and Mouse**

Accessibility: ★★★★

Since the Call of Duty series added player rankings in 2006, it's become a huge multiplayer title, and 2018's Call of Duty: Black Ops IIII made the bold choice of ditching the single-player campaign altogether, opting for Blackout, a Fortnite-style Battle Royale mode instead.

## Trivia

The lack of a single-player campaign drew some ire from fans, who felt disappointed by its absence. Co-studio head Dan Bunting pushed back in interviews though, claiming "We are delivering so much more of what players spend most of their time doing in our games in the series." Or to put it another way, no-one played the single player campaigns anyway.

## BLOP to the Future

Black Ops IIII has been explicitly designed with eSports in mind, and the developers have added spectator modes too, with the mandate that it should be as fun and easy to watch as it is to play. It introduced the World League Hub, a section of the game explicitly focussed on eSports, to help you track your progression. With the addition of regular league events and a pro series, it seems like the Call of Duty team are taking eSports very seriously indeed.

# Load Up On Guns

There's a lot of great firepower to be had in Call of Duty: Black Ops IIII. We've picked out some of the more... interesting weapons you can expect to find...

**DEATH RAY**
**First Appearance:** Call of Duty: World At War
**Magazine Size:** 20 Shots
**Ammunition:** 20+160
**Info:** Nothing gives you that retro sci-fi vibe like the ray gun. Developed by Dr. Ludvig Maxis from Group 395, this cold fusion powered weapon shoots out green circular lasers. Pew pew!

**CYMBAL MONKEY**
**First Appearance:** Call of Duty: World At War
**Magazine Size:** N/A
**Ammunition:** 3
**Info:** Just look at its evil monkey face! Not silent, but definitely deadly, the cymbal monkey makes a ton of noise before exploding - perfect for luring in unsuspecting zombies.

**DEATH OF ORION**
**First Appearance:** Call of Duty: Black Ops IIII
**Magazine Size:** 1 Shot
**Ammunition:** 1+45
**Info:** Ok, who wouldn't want to go into battle with a magical scorpion attached to a trigger mechanism? It may initially seem like a slow semi-automatic, but it has a sting in its tail – charging the shot releases a capture beam that can ensnare players and anyone in their immediate vicinity.

# Top Competition

**Name:** Doritos Bowl 2018 ● **Location:** San Jose, California
**Prize Pool:** $250,000 ● **Description:** The first major tournament since the game's launch, the 2018 Doritos Bowl at TwitchCon 2018 saw Team Shroud beating everyone off to take the top prize of $100,000.

# HEARTHSTONE

Probably the most popular collectable card game around today, Hearthstone was initially a smaller project to go alongside Blizzard's mega franchises like World of Warcraft and Starcraft. It was an instant obsession for gamers, and the game has had numerous expansions and tweaks since release.

Year of release: **2014**

Developer: **Blizzard Entertainment**

eSports platform: **PC/ Mac OS/iOS/Android**

Team or solo play: **Solo**

Average match length: **5 - 10 mins**

Play method: **Mouse/Touch**

Accessibility: ★★★★★

## Trivia

A cheating scandal erupted at the 2014 DreamHack Summer tournament event in Sweden, when Radu "Rdu" Dima received a Battle.Net message during a match detailing the contents of his opponent's hand. Upset by the message, Radu called a halt to proceedings as organisers tried to work out how to proceed. Luckily, the message was redundant, as play had already progressed beyond that point, and it was decided by both players that play could continue. Radu went on to win the match, and first prize of $10,000.

## No Hearth Measures

The first ever competition, the Hearthstone Innkeeper's Invitational taking place at BlizzCon in November 2013, took place more than four months before the game's official launch. Since then, in addition to many smaller tournaments, Blizzard has held the Hearthstone World Championships annually, usually at BlizzCon. If you want to compete at this level be prepared to spend a lot of time playing - and opening card packs!

# How to Play

Every Hearthstone match takes place on a board very similar to this one. Here we'll take you through some of the basics.

1. **This is your character. You can choose from many different classes. The number in the bottom right is your hit points. If these fall to zero, you lose the match!**

2. **This is your opponent. Again, the number in the bottom right represents his hit points. If these fall to zero, you win the match!**

3. **These are your starting cards. If you select a card, you can see its attributes, including its attack and defence stats, as well as any special abilities. The number in the top left is how much mana the card costs to play.**

4. **This is your mana pool. It increases each round, unlocking stronger cards and more gameplay options.**

5. **This is your Hero Power. This is your character's unique special ability.**

6. **This is where you'll see your currently deployed units, and you can see your opponent's units on the other half of the play field. In most cases, you'll need to get rid of the opposing units before you can take on your opponent.**

# Top Competition

**Name:** Hearthstone World Championships ● **Location:** Various
**Prize Pool:** $1m ● **Description:** The Hearthstone World Championships are held by Blizzard annually. Just 16 players get to take part, so the competition is fierce. It's not easy to get a seat by the hearth either - players must earn enough Hearthstone Championship Tour (HCT) points to be eligible, available at various tournaments around the world.

# GAMES 11-15

### « StarCraft II »

**Year of release:** 2010 ● **Developer:** Blizzard
Entertainment ● **eSports platform:** PC/Mac OS ●
**Team or solo play:** Solo ● **Average match length:**
10 - 15 mins ● **Play method:** Keyboard and mouse
● **Accessibility:** ★★★

StarCraft II is almost a decade old now, but it's
still an eSports juggernaut, particularly in South
Korea, where matches are televised, it's players
are national celebrities and thousands of fans fill
stadiums for tournaments. Internationally it's still
extremely popular, and the game was one of
the few games to be chosen as an event in the
2018 Asian Games.

### « Counter Strike: Global Offensive

**Year of release:** 2012 ● **Developer:**
Hidden Path Entertainment ● **eSports
platform:** PC ● **Also Available On:**
Mac OS/Xbox 360/PS3 ● **Team or solo
play:** Team ● **Average match length:**
10 - 15 mins ● **Play method:** Keyboard
and mouse ● **Accessibility:** ★★★

The appeal of Counter Strike is
immediate – playing as either a team
of terrorists or counter-terrorists, each
group must work together to thwart
their opposition. Counter Strike: Global
Offensive (Usually abbreviated to CS:
GO) is the most recent incarnation,
and there are regular pro tournaments
(known as Majors) where teams can
test their skills.

# F1 2018 »

**Year of release:** 2018 ● **Developer:**
Codemasters ● **eSports platform:** PC
● **Also available on:** Xbox One/PS4/
iOS/Android ● **Team or solo play:**
Solo ● **Average match length:** 1hr
● **Play method:** Steering Wheel
● **Accessibility:** ★★

Although there have been licensed
F1 games since video games
began, it was Codemasters' F1
2017 game that brought Formula
1 to eSports, with the launch of the Formula 1 eSports
series. The first winner was Brit Brendon Leigh, who lifted the
champagne in October 2017 at the Gfinity Arena in London.

# « Heroes of the Storm

**Year of release:** 2015
● **Developer:** Blizzard Entertainment
● **eSports platform:** PC/Mac OS ● **Team or solo
Play:** Team ● **Average match length:** 20 - 30 minutes ●
**Play method:** Keyboard and mouse ● **Accessibility:** ★★★

An attempt by Blizzard Entertainment to take on the character-based
Multiplayer Online Battle Arena (MOBA) genre, Heroes of the Storm managed
to carve out its own space in the eSports world, but it never quite gained the
mass appeal of League of Legends.

# PlayerUnknown Battlegrounds »

**Year of release:** 2017 ● **Developer:** PUBG
Corporation ● **eSports platform:** PC ● **Also
available on:** PS4/Xbox One/Android/iOS
● **Team or solo play:** Solo/Team ● **Average match
length:** 30 - 40 mins ● **Play method:** Keyboard and
Mouse ● **Accessibility:** ★★★★★

Debuting a few months before Fortnite,
PlayerUnknown's Battlegrounds (better known
as PUBG) was responsible for creating the
Battle Royale format that is now being copied
everywhere. Tournaments are definitely starting to
appear, so this could be fertile ground for pro gamers.

# GAMES 16-20

## Dota 2

**Year of release:** 2009 ● **Developer:** Valve Corporation ●
**eSports platform:** PC/Mac OS ● **Team or solo play:**
Team ● **Average match length:** 35 - 45 mins ● **Play
method:** Keyboard and mouse
● **Accessibility:** ★★★

Defense of the Ancients was an extremely
popular Warcraft mod that essentially created
the Multiplayer Online Battle Arena (MOBA)
genre. Noticing that its employees were
spending more time playing DotA than
working, Half-Life creators Valve Corporation
developed Dota 2 as a sequel, enlisting Ice Frog,
one of DotA's longest serving designers to help
develop the game. Dota 2 has gone on to become
one of the biggest games in the eSports world.

## Halo 5: Guardians ⌃

**Year of release:** 2015 ● **Developer:** 343 Industries ● **eSports
platform:** Xbox One ● **Team or solo play:** Team ● **Average match
length:** 12 mins ● **Play method:** Gamepad ● **Accessibility:** ★★★★★

Halo 5: Guardians may have got some stick over its short single-
player campaign, but the multiplayer game is a classic. It's one of
the reasons it's still played at tournament level, and the Halo World
Championship 2018 saw 16 teams of 4 Halo players battle it out for
supremacy for a slice of the $1 million prize pot. US Team Splyce
took the crown - not bad for a team that was barely a year old.

## World of Tanks

**Year of release:** 2010 ● **Developer:** Wargaming Minsk ● **eSports platform:** PC/Xbox One/PS4 ● **Team or solo play:** Team ● **Average match length:** 30m - 1hr ● **Play method:** Keyboard and mouse
● **Accessibility:** ★★★★

Coming out of Belarus in 2010, World of Tanks is a premium freeplay game that has grown exponentially in popularity since its debut. It entered the world of eSports in 2012 at the World Cyber Games, and has had many subsequent tournaments. After the 2017 Grand Finals, 2018 saw Wargaming re-think their approach to eSports - a new format is expected to be unveiled soon.

## Warcraft III ≫

**Year of release:** 2002 ● **Developer:** Blizzard Entertainment
● **eSports platform:** PC ● **Team or solo play:** Solo ● **Average match length:** 15 - 20 mins ● **Play method:** Keyboard and mouse
● **Accessibility:** ★★★

Warcraft III is the grandaddy of the eSports scene. One of the earliest games to reach its potential as a spectator sport, Warcraft III became extremely popular in South Korea. Its popularity has waned significantly since 2010, but tournaments still take place, and legendary players like five time World Champion Moon are still active on the scene.

## Clash Royale

**Year of release:** 2016 ● **Developer:** Supercell ● **eSports platform:** iOS/Android
● **Team or solo play:** Solo/team ● **Average match length:** 3 - 5 mins ● **Play method:** Touch ● **Accessibility:** ★★★★

Designed as a spinoff from Supercell's massively popular Clash of Clans series, Clash Royale combines elements from both Collectible Card Games and Multiplayer Online Battle Arenas to create something heady and new. It was a success too, generating over $1 billion in revenue in its first year. Designed to be played in short sessions, this is the ideal game for those who like gaming on the move.

# GLOSSARY

**AGGRO** A way of drawing enemies to a single teammate, usually your tank.

**AOE** Area of Effect – the radius of damage that will be caused by a particular spell or ability.

**AUTO ATTACK** An attack that can be made to deploy over and over again, usually at no or little cost.

**BM** Bad Manners.

**BRUSH** A hiding spot.

**BUFF** A power increase or decrease that can be aimed at a player or a team.

**BUILD** The way your character has been tweaked for a certain performance focus.

**BURST DAMAGE** Abilities or weapons that deal massive amounts of damage extremely quickly.

**CARRY** A protected player.

**CASTING** Can refer to either match commentating or a spell cast.

**CC** Crowd control. Any ability that stops you from being overwhelmed by mobs. These can include knockbacks, stuns or blinds.

**CCG** A Collectable Card Game.

**CHEESE** Dirty tricks used to win a match.

**COMP** Composition – the characters your team is composed of.

**COOLDOWN** The length of time before an ability or weapon can be used again.

**CS** Creep Score – the amount of NPC's you've taken down in a match.

**DENYING** The art of preventing the opposition from killing a mob or a team-mate.

**DIVE** Moving into an area densely populated by the opposition to grab kills.

**DPS** Damage Per Second – a way to compare character builds, weapons or abilities that takes into account the differing speeds of various attack types.

**DQ** Disqualified – try not to get this one.

**DRAFTING** A process that allows players to pick their characters before a match.

**FARM** A way to amass large amounts of gold during a match.

**FF** Finish Fast – can either be a signal to team mates that you're ready to win, or a plea to the opposition to end a losing match quickly

**FLAMING** Harassing or insulting other players.

**FOG OF WAR** An area of the map which is hidden from view.

**FPS** First Person Shooter – any shooting game where you view the action from the character's point of view.

**FRAG** A kill.

**GANKING** Essentially, stabbing someone in the back.

**GG** Good Game - usually used at the end of a match to demonstrate sportsmanship.

**GLASS CANNON** A powerful character that has an extremely weak defense.

**GLHF** Good Luck Have Fun – usually said at the start of a match.

**GOLD ADVANTAGE** The team with the most gold.

**GRIEFING** A deliberate attempt to infuriate other players.

**HARASS/POKE** Using small attacks from a distance to weaken an enemy.

**INITIATING** Starting a fight.

**JUKE** Baiting a player to move in a certain direction.

**JUNGLER** A player who focuses more on taking out NPC's than the opposing players.

**KDA** Kills, Deaths and Assists – an ingame scoreboard that keeps track of how everyone's doing.

**KITING** Encouraging an enemy to chase you, while staying out of reach.

**LANING** Used in MOBA's to describe the process of running down a lane to farm and fight in the early portion of the game.

**LAST HIT** The killing blow.

**META** Short for Metagame, meta refers to current build trends, and is most often used in Collectable Card Games like Hearthstone.

**MINIONS/CREEPS** Another term for Mobs.

**MMORPG** A Massively Multiplayer Online Role Playing Game.

**MOB** An enemy character.

**MOBA** Multiplayer Online Battle Arena.

**NERF** When the game developer reduces the power of a character, weapon or ability, to re-balance the game.

**NPC** Non-Player Character – any character not controlled by any of the players.

**OBJECTIVE** A goal that you must achieve.

**OOM** Out Of Mana – used when a player can no longer use their abilities due to a lack of Mana.

**PEEL** Ending the current activity to help a team-mate.

**PUBG** Short for PlayerUnknown Battlegrounds.

**PUSH** A command for your team to move forward and attack the next set of targets.

**QQ** A flame encouraging your opponent to quit (or occasionally, cry).

**RECALL** Teleporting across the map.

**RNG** Random Number Generation - refers to anything that has an element of randomness to it, like the items received when opening a chest for example.

**RTS** Real Time Strategy - strategy games that don't feature turn-based gameplay.

**RUSH** Attacking your opponents quickly before they have a chance to build up their defenses.

**SALTY** Used to describe an upset opponent.

**SHOTCALLER** The person on the team who calls the shots, usually the team leader.

**SMOKE** Any item or weapon that obscures the opposition's view.

**SNOWBALL** When a team has become so powerful that their opponents are unable to deal with them.

**TANK** Any character that can soak up a lot of damage, for example Winston in Overwatch.

**TILT** A player that is playing badly, usually due to anger.

**ULTIMATE** Any character's ultimate ability.

**VISION** How much of the map you can see.

**XP** Experience Points.

**ZERG** Also known as a Zerg Rush, after its popular use in StarCraft II matches, this is any cheap tactic that relies on overwhelming the opposing player extremely quickly.

**ZONING** Using aggression to force an opponent out of an area.

# INDEX

# ABOUT THE AUTHOR

**JON HAMBLIN** is a games industry veteran, after making his start in the QA department of Sega in 2000. Since then, he's written for a raft of publications, including Edge, The Guardian, PlayStation Official Magazine UK, SFX and Gamesmaster. He's also an award-winning games producer, and has created games for Disney, Cartoon Network and the BBC. He currently lives in South London with his cat Nala.